WOMEN OF THE MILITARY

A Compilation of the Stories of
American Service Women

Interviews collected and compiled by Amanda Huffman

Dedication

For my husband and my boys.

For all the women who have served, are currently serve or will one day serve in the military. Your stories make this book possible you encourage and inspire me every day.

ISBN numbers
978-1-7331765-0-7 (ebook)
978-1-7331765-1-4 (kindle)
978-1-7331765-2-1 (hard copy)
978-1-0793284-4-8 (edition 1)

Acknowledgements

This book idea came after my 31 Day Deployment Story series. It was there that women shared their experience of being deployed in the military. The challenges they faced. The things they did. It was inspiring. From there, an idea to focus on women was sparked. Thank you to those first initial women who shared their story for the deployment series. I owe you a book as well and hope to put your stories together in the near future. This book wouldn't be possible without the stories from the amazing women who were willing to share their experience. This book would not exist without their stories. Stories that encouraged and inspired me to share them with the world. Thank you to my mom for helping edit the countless pages and so many of the blog posts I have written for my blog and other guest articles and blogs.

To my mom who spent timeless hours editing not only this book, but so many of the blog posts I have written for my blog, guest blogs and publications. I appreciate everything you have done to help me and appreciate your support.

To my husband for supporting me on my crazy blogging adventure that has turned into a passion project. Your support means so much to me.

And to my boys. I left the military behind to be a stay at home mom and you have made the transition worth all the heartache and pain. I love getting to be your mom and love that I can work while being there for these early moments that won't last long enough.

**I am grateful for the following supporters whose preorders
and contributions helped to make this book possible:**

Alison Wang

Jen Zetterstrom

Dawn Gomillion

Maureen Elias

Desiray Tuinstra

The Ward Family, Joe, Becky, Fiona and Aidan

Faith Haren

Women of the Military Book Sponsors:

Praise for Women of the Military

My favorite part of reading Women of the Military has been diving into the stories. While I may be a military spouse, I do not know what it is to be a woman in uniform or raise my hand in a pledge of service to my country. I have been surprised, challenged, and enlightened by the stories within Amanda's book. I have a daughter, and in reading Amanda's book I now have something to pass on to her when she is old enough to question if military service might be a good fit/pursuit for her.

- Lindsay, Military Spouse and Mom

This is a fabulous collection of inspirational stories of endurance, struggles, and women forging their own futures. The diversity of their backgrounds and experiences is fascinating but the broad range of military careers is astounding and sets to heart how integral women are in the military.

This is a must read for anyone considering a career with the armed forces or struggling to figure out their future careers. The challenges and adjustments these women have made to create the life best suited for them is the type of motivational encouragement that can help others be confident in reaching their dreams.

- Natalie, US Air Force Veteran

You may have been deeply inspired after watching Netflix's Medal of Honor (2018) or standing below a breathtaking firework display on the 4th of July. Rightly so. Our service members deserve to be recognized and applauded.

Yet, many of their stories remain unknown. American soldiers rapidly join from mixed backgrounds and genders- all of which are significant to our country's protection. Since 1948 (when Congress permitted women to serve in the US military), hundreds of boots have been worn, shots have been fired, and wars have been won due to female influence.

But you haven't heard of them.

Amanda's interviews represent today's highly diverse, female demographic in national defense. They boldly share real, unedited experiences from Navy, Marine, Air Force, and Army perspectives. Stop Googling what it's like to do basic training, get through school or leave your family. You're about to find out."

- Faith, supporter of military women

Table of Contents

INTRODUCTION

In 2017, I set out on a journey to share the stories of men and women who had deployed. I started with two stories from World War II. One I had heard growing up when my neighbor would talk about how he had survived World War II. The stories increased when I decided to join the military. And though he is no longer with us, I still own the tape recording he gave me when I was a junior in high school. I also had a copy of the story my Great Uncle Ray showed me after he found out I was joining the Air Force. He survived Pearl Harbor and had his story written in a book compiling all the stories of these great men.

I also had my own deployment story to tell.

I embarked on a journey to tell deployment stories in the month of October as part of a 31 Day Series called Write 31 Days. I emailed men and women who deployed with me. I emailed friends who I knew had deployed or their husbands had deployed. I sent surveys out on various Facebook group and in the end, I ended up with a group of stories of mostly military women sharing their experience of deploying.

The stories I heard captivated me and inspired me. And I planned to do a follow up series in 2018 focused on military women. But life happened and the series didn't happen in October. So, I decided to take the stories I had collected and put them together here in this book.

28 military experiences from women. Three women about to embark on their own military journey. fifteen Air Force, eight Army, one Navy and one Marine.

Stories that will encourage you, inspire you and maybe make you cry. Join me on a journey to not only learn about the service of these women but how it changed their life forever.

Thank you to everyone who was willing to share their story for this book. I am forever in your debt.

A NEW AIR FORCE ADVENTURE

*M*ariah is currently a military spouse in the process of join-ing the United States Air Force. She met her now husband in high school. They were great friends and then when he left for the military everything changed and she decided she wanted to follow him on his military adventure. It was a lengthy pro-cess to joining the military. She leaves for Basic Training (aka Boot Camp) in mid-June of 2019.

What was your journey to military life?

My journey was interesting. I have had a few family members join the military and my best friend's sister married into the military. I always told myself that I could never do that, that I need someone to be here with me. But that all changed after my now husband went to Basic Military Training (BMT) or boot camp. I had realized that he was the only person that I would be willing to do this crazy life for. So, we talked it over, he came home on leave and we decided to start dating. We already knew at this point that we would start a life together. After that I planned a trip to visit him in San Antonio. A month later I found myself packing my bags, saying my goodbyes, and driving from California to Texas to start my new life.

What is your favorite part of being a military spouse?

My favorite part of being a military spouse is getting out and ex-ploring where my husband is stationed. I honestly haven't done much as a military spouse when it comes to being involved with other military spouses.

What is the hardest part of being a military spouse?

Originally the hardest part was adjusting to my husband's work schedule and the random "oh hey I have training on this day".

Now, the hardest part of being a military spouse is definitely not having my friends and family here. I have close family members who have medical issues, I missed my best friend getting engaged, and I'm missing the first few years of my first niece growing up. But I knew things would happen and they thankfully all understand.

What is the best place you have lived and why?

We have only been in San Antonio, so I guess San Antonio! It is actually really cool that my husband is stationed where everyone gets their start in the Air Force. I have had the opportunity to attend some graduations and it is incredible. The San Antonio area itself is not my favorite (my husband and I are from a small country town, so it is the complete opposite) but the surrounding areas are incredible. It's awesome when we have time to get out and explore.

Did you ever consider joining the military before becoming a military spouse?

I have wanted to join the military since 4th grade (I am finishing up my sophomore year of college) but never knew which branch I wanted to join. Being with my husband and seeing his base has helped me understand which branch I want, and which branch is the best fit.

Why do you want to join the military?

I want to join the military because this country has given me so much. My faith is very important to me and I know that many countries people are not allowed to express their faith freely. I also want to join because I have family members who have served or are currently serving. For me, joining would not be about any of the benefits that come with it.

It would be about me supporting my country and all those before me, currently, and in the future that are making the sacrifice to help keep the country the way it is.

How do you think life will change as a military member compared to a military spouse?

I definitely think life will be harder. Since I'm only a civilian, I cannot understand how hard it really will be, so I understand as much as someone in my position possibly can. Some of the things I have gone through as a military spouse has kind of helped me get ready.

What career field are you hoping to join? And why?

I'm really hoping to get a job in munitions. I'm a very hands on person and I feel like with munitions, it will give me enough of a challenge, but not too much of a challenge like my husband's career. Of course, I'm realistic and know that I may not get that job, so I have about seven others written down. But Munitions is the career field I really want.

What excites you the most about joining the military?

I have some silly things and then some serious things that excite me. My silly things are I can't wait to see my last name on my chest, along with "US Air Force". My husband and I also joke around that it will be kind of cool to have another "Trainee Hammond" even though I know the second that is yelled at me I will never want it yelled at me again!

Another silly thing is how Military Entrance Processing Station (MEPS, where you get your military physical done) has put me on a hold for my physical until October, so it will be so rewarding to get in after waiting over a year. The MEPS process took until end of April to clear me to enter the delayed entry program into the Air Force. Now I am waiting for boot camp later this year.

The serious things are how I just can't wait to serve my country. I can't wait to stand alongside not just my husband, but everyone else who is making the sacrifice. I am also excited to be able

Amanda Huffman

to experience everything that my husband went through, we kind of came to the conclusion that it should help me understand his life a little better. I am also very excited to possibly explore places, because I'll have a different job than my husband so we're hoping it'll take us to a new place.

*E*mileigh started her United States Air Force adventure as a military spouse. She and her husband are now both serving in the Air Force. He is a Chaplain and she is a Public Affairs officer. She shared part of her story weeks before she left for Total Force Officer Training (TFOT) in Alabama. And I was able to get a few follow up questions to update her story a year after she went on active duty. You can follow her and her husband's Air Force adventure on their blog Lead with the Left.

Why did you decide to join the Air Force?

I've wanted to join the military since I was about twelve. This was confirmed later when I got to experience living in countries that are not free. I saw how valuable the freedoms we have in America are, and I know it's worth the price to protect those. As for the Air Force specifically, my husband had just enlisted in the Air Force when I met him, and I've seen his positive experiences throughout the years. It seemed most sustainable for us long-term as a couple as we'd both like to give military careers a shot.

What do you hope to learn from joining the military?

I know I'll learn *so* much. The things I'm most excited about are developing my leadership and war skills.

What do you think military life will be like?

I've gotten a taste of it as a spouse, and I know it will include a lot of adapting and making do with the circumstances we've got. I am excited for the opportunity to see what I'm made of and to support the military community with my husband in his future chaplaincy ministry.

What career field did you pick and why?

I chose (and happily received) an assignment to Public Affairs. It fits well with my multicultural experience from living overseas as a teenager and my undergrad degree of multicultural studies. I enjoy learning languages and interacting with those from other cultures as well as the strategic and political ramifications of communication.

What do you think will be the hardest part of military life?

I think the general learning curve will be difficult at first along with being a dual military couple and figuring out our career progressions. However, I'm confident in the strength of our marriage and the network of mentors we've built.

What are you doing to prepare to attend your officer training school?

I've borrowed my husband's training materials from Commissioned Officer Training (COT) a different commissioning program that he attended the summer before I joined (the coursework is pretty much the same) as well as working out a lot to prepare for the fitness standards. Jacob, my husband, has also helped me with marching, saluting, facing movements, etc.

Are you worried about any part of military life?

Honestly, no. We're Christians and we've seen God's provision and help at every stage of our journey so far. We know He's called us to be where we are and will equip and help us to thrive in military life.

What is one thing you hope to accomplish while serving in the military?

I hope to set a good example of integrous leadership, particularly for military females. There aren't as many out there, and there is still new ground to break as far as our roles and treatment in the military. Jacob and I also hope to show others what a healthy dual military marriage can be and how to live out commitment for the long haul.

Who do you admire and why?

I really admire Gen. Ann Dunwoody. I read her book "A Higher Standard" recently, and I was inspired by her personal journey and in being a "first woman" to do a lot of things. She encountered obstacles, but her hard work and attitude led her to become the first female four-star general in the US military. When people didn't believe in her or believe a woman should be doing something, she ignored their remarks and did it anyway, often earning their respect in the process.

What is it like to join the military when your husband is already serving?

So far, it's actually been pretty great. I have someone to help me understand the system and culture of the military. It's allowed me to get on military bases in order to buy uniforms before training. It's also handy that both of us understand what it's like to leave *and* what it's like to be left. I help him prepare to hold down the home front, and he helps me prepare for training. I don't have to be worried about him while I'm gone because I know he understands what I'm experiencing and won't be upset if, for example, I can't call him often.

What was your officer commissioning program (TFOT) like?

TFOT was actually a couple of the most fun months of my life! I was sleep deprived and it was challenging, but I was finally getting the chance to earn my place in the military, a years-long dream I've had. I had an amazing flight, most of whom were prior-enlisted, and flight commander who helped me develop my leadership and think through what it means to be "Lieutenant Rogers."

What is active duty military life like?

I am exactly one year into Active Duty life as of today, May,

24 2019! It has been one of the most challenging and learning-filled years of my life. Particularly in my job as a Public Affairs Officer, a lot of my day-to-day work is very visible to wing leadership and the public, so I have learned to deal with pressure and navigate military hierarchy. It's still very much a learning process. One year in, I mostly realize how much I do not know and how great my job really is. I'm comforted by the fact that I have grown a lot, and I'm sure several years down the road I will be a very capable person!

You are a Public Affairs officer, what training did that require and what are you doing today?

Our tech school is at the joint Defense Information School at Fort Meade near Washington, D.C. The initial tech school stint is about two months long, but the vast majority of my training has come on the job, learning through experience and by networking with other Public Affairs (PA) Officers that are further down the road than I am. Currently I work at a base PA shop as one of two officers, and I run Media Operations, working with civilian media agencies. A lot of my job is researching, analyzing, and trusting my gut to make the right decision or to advise commanders with the best plan on how to engage with media or get a narrative to the public. Since we work with people, very few things are black and white.

You are pregnant with your first child, what are you doing to prepare for mil to mil life with a baby?

My husband, Jacob, will be an Individual Mobilized Augmentee (IMA) Reservist for a while and the main caregiver for our baby after she is born. We decided to do it this way rather than getting Jacob onto Active Duty immediately because it gives us a bit more margin to figure career and life things out before both of us are Active.

I have also joined some social media groups specific to women officers, dual military couples, and military moms. This internet group of women has been a HUGE source of knowledge and insight on how to navigate regulations, work issues, leadership challenges, and parenting in a military context.

J *oan Olsen (Adams) was first female cadet to be sworn into the Air Force Academy. The class of 1980 (starting in 1976) had something no other class before it had. It had women. 156 cadets of the cadets who attend the Air Force Academy starting the summer of 1976 were women. The first class to allow women to attend the Air Force Academy. Out of those 156 women 97 commissioned. Joan was only at the Academy for 9 months, and hearing the story puts the context of how hard it was for women to attend and graduate from the Air Force Academy. Joan didn't graduate, but the Academy is how she met her husband and after they were married, he Enlisted in the military and they eventually ended up in Los Angeles where she had a successful career with Raytheon.*

Why did you decide to join the Air Force?

I don't recall a conscious decision to join the Air Force. Growing up, my father always took us to the base open houses and air-shows near the areas we were living. He was a Korean War veteran in the Air Force for one tour. He always had a fondness of the Air Force and wishes he had made it his career.

What made you consider attending the Air Force Academy?

I was looking for college scholarship opportunities. My parents were not well off and did not have college funds for us kids. I was a high achiever in high school in math and science. I always assumed I would go to college and the Reserve Officer Training Corps (ROTC) was high on my list of places to go for a scholarship. Student loans and low-cost tuition at California junior colleges did not really exist. My father followed the news a lot. Congress was in the process of passing legislation to admit women [to the service academies] a year before I graduated from high school. The application processes were all put in place in 1975 waiting for the legislation to become law.

What was the process like to join the Air Force Academy?

You have to have a nomination from a Congressman to be considered. Each legislator gets a certain number of the two types of nominations for each service academy. So, the process involved researching what nominations my Representative and Senators had open and to what academies. There are two types of nominations that they can grant, competitive and principle (no competition). The legislators had an application process as well as the academies. I applied to United States Air Force Academy (USAFA) and Annapolis (Navy Academy) and then waited to see what came through on nominations. Grades, Scholastic Aptitude Test (SAT) scores, written essays, and extracurricular activities were all considered. I received two nominations to USAFA. One competitive from one of the Senators (I can't remember which one – Cranston or Tunney), and a principle from my Representative, John Moss (CA 3rd district, Sacramento). The principle nomination secured a place for me in the class of 1980. The process after is a blur but somewhat like enlisting – physical testing mostly. The local papers carried a story or two.

You were one of the 156 women in the first class to allow women to attend the Air Force Academy. What was it like to be in culture that had once not been open to women?

Before the class of 1980 got there, the Air Force decided to bring in 15 female junior officers to serve as surrogate cadets to train the guys and to be "upper class" surrogates to the freshman women. They didn't perform well and created an atmosphere before we got there where the upper-class cadets assumed the freshman females would be no better. Many of the squadron chants were changed to remove sexual references which created some hard feelings. Our fellow classmates felt as though we were taking spots away from the guys and wanted nothing to do with us. It was quite tense and untested ground for everyone. The officers leading the squadrons (the Air Officer Commanding's (AOCs)) were looking for and exploiting any weakness (physically or academically).

What was your first few weeks at the Air Force Academy like?

The first day was induction. Say good-bye to your family. Haircuts, uniform/equipment issue, squadron/room assignments, vaccinations, learning to drill, how to address your upperclassmen, how to carry your demilitarized M-1, etc. Lots of yelling and insults. First lesson in how to create a stone face. Learning how to act and eat in the mess hall. Essentially the first day of basic training.

A news crew followed me around that day since I was the first of the first class. There are a lot of YouTube videos now that show what the first day of being a USAFA cadet is like. The end of the first day you get to see your family one last time. Then basic training starts.

PT, reading and memorizing the USAFA knowledge book called Contrails, more "education" on how to act/recite under pressure, how to fill out the daily mess hall survey, on and on and on. After the first 3 weeks, you get to march from your dorm room out to a dusty bivouac in Jack's Valley for combat drill, orienteering, obstacle course, bayonet assault course, leadership reaction course, combat arms training (M-16), etc.

I badly sprained both ankles in Jack's Valley. During the "run" on the last day there, someone finally relieved my agony when I was stopped while limping the course and was sent to the infirmary for treatment (which lasted about 2 months).

I received dozens of letters from people across the country about 50/50 encouraging/discouraging or angry. I was featured on a "CBS: In the News" segment which they used to air between programs.

How long did you attend the Air Force Academy?

I was there from June 1976 through Feb 1977. Basic training plus one semester (21.5 semester hours) of classes.

What caused you to leave the Air Force Academy without commissioning?

Earlier I mentioned that the AOC's were looking for weaknesses. Mine turned out to be academics (math in particular). 21.5 semester hours was an insane school load. These were the days before personal computers. My only technology was an issued basic calculator by today's standards. Papers were done on typewriters. I was placed in calculus and failed the class.

My issue was that I was weak in trigonometry which I found out later (when I went back to college) was essential for calculus. I believe the AOC and all of your professors had a say in whether you should stay or go. My calculus professor voted stay. The other prof's whose classes I passed and the AOC voted go. I was academically disenrolled. No discussion, no appeal. Others that fail classes are allowed to repeat and then catch up with their classmates over the summer.

I have to say I was relieved but also devastated at the time and giving the news to my father was particularly painful. There's an opportunity to repeat the class outside of the halls of USAFA and then apply to be readmitted but then you are in a different class. I don't think many people have done this. They tell cadets while they are there that even if they don't have great grades, that after the academy, any graduate school will give them consideration for admission because it was such a tough school. One of the biggest fabrications I've ever heard.

I pretty much hated most of my short time as a cadet. I'd say I was an adequate cadet but I didn't have a passion for it. It wasn't the life for me.

How did your military training at the Air Force Academy affect the rest of your life?

The training gave me a unique insight into a man's world. The expectation that you don't fall apart under pressure or personal insult. Training in how to hide or repress your feelings. Training in how to not take things too personally. Training in how to assess and solve problems, remember details, absorb information. Training in how to adapt and overcome your weaknesses. Recognizing BS from reality. It definitely prepared me to enter the world of engineering at an aerospace company where women were few at the time.

What did you do after leaving the Air Force Academy?

Worked at Sears and a savings and loan. Got married. Accompanied my husband to his assignments. We lived like paupers for 7 years (I was working at KFC, Base Exchange (BX), commissary (on base grocery store)) during the Carter years. My husband had a 2nd job at McDonald's. I went back to school during the Reagan years (got straight A's in math from trigonometry to calculus to linear equations). Got an Electrical Engineering Degree with Honors from California State Sacramento in 1985. Then I went to work for Hughes Aircraft/GM Hughes/Raytheon. Spent the next 28.5 years there. Retired in 2013. My husband retired from the Air Force in 1998.

How did you meet your husband?

My husband was a sophomore at the academy. We met when we were traveling home for Thanksgiving break 1976. His family lived in Lodi and mine was in Elk Grove, about 20 miles apart. We just hit it off talking. When I was disenrolled, he took an active interest in me and a romance bloomed. Our first dance was at the academy Valentine's Ball. I left soon after that and he left at the end of his sophomore year. We figured we could make a life together without the military. That was a pipe dream in the Carter years and you can't really make a career in the meat packing business. So, he enlisted and that journey began for us. We got engaged in 1977 and married in 1978.

What was it like to be a military spouse?

When my husband first re-joined the Air Force, it was very hard. The economy was horrible. Inflation was between 10-15%. When we moved to Tyndall Air Force Base after tech school in Denver, we barely had enough money to make ends meet ($5 between paychecks). Until he made enough rank, we couldn't even get base housing. Lots of coupon clipping, meal planning, aluminum recycling, etc. We couldn't get credit.

Jobs were hard to come by for me. Panama City was very depressed and depressing. I had part time jobs for the most part

(KFC, BX, commissary). After several years of applying, my husband was selected for Air Education Training and Command and we went to Sacramento to finish college (E-5 rank went with that). We lived on Mather AFB. The Air Force essentially paid for both of us to finish school. After that, he went to Officer Training School then we got assigned to Los Angeles AFB while I finished my last semester of college and looked for a job in LA.

He spent his 13-year officer career in Los Angeles (LA) (with the exception of Squadron Officer School in residence). He made Permeant Change of Stations a lot but always in LA (Global Positioning System (GPS), school, Defense Logistics Agency (DLA), launch, Mil-Sat-Comm). There were freezes on assignments and Reduction in Forces (RIFs) going on. There were no deployments during his time in the Air Force so, there was only separation for OTS, SOS, and Temporary Duty (TDYs). He was selected for an Air Force Institute of Technology – Civilian Institute (AFIT-CI) program for a master's degree in Electrical Engineering at University of Southern California. No children entered into the picture so, I put my head down and had a career at Hughes/Raytheon.

All that being said, I loved being an Air Force wife. We made lifelong friends at every assignment. People we are still involved with to this day. I have no regrets and wouldn't trade my life for another.

What would you tell girls considering attending the Air Force Academy?

I would tell them that it could be the most challenging and rewarding thing they could choose to do. It's not for everybody but it's hard to know until you go. I had a discussion like that with a young girl living on my street at the time I was a cadet. Many years later, I was at a Mil-Sat-Comm Christmas party talking with the wife of one of my husband's teammates on the unit softball team. She was a stay at home mom, but had been a KC-135 pilot during Desert Storm. She had gone to and graduated from USAFA and trained to be a pilot afterwards. She decided to go to the Academy after talking to a cadet home for a break. After inquiring where she grew up, the cadet she talked to turned out to be me. Gave me chills.

*B*efore leaving for Basic Training I was able to talk to Leia*
about her experience of why she wanted to join the military.
I loved hearing her story and it reminded me of the days leading up to me joining the Reserve Officer Training Program.

Why did you decide to join the Air Force?

I joined the Air Force primarily because I was tired of riding the
merry-go-round of college. I would throw my heart and soul
into one career choice after another, but never found something
that resonated with me. Additionally, I wanted to carry on the
family legacy, as my Grandfather and Father served in the Air
Force.

What do you hope to learn from joining the military?

By joining the military, I simply hope to become a better version of myself, so I can better serve those around me. I would
like to learn what it takes to run a high-risk operation. I am
eager to get a firsthand perspective on government issues and
military structure. I look forward to working alongside service-
members from other branches and better understanding what
'sacrifice' truly means. I would also like to become competent
at handling firearms and highly disciplined in my career.

What do you think military life will be like?

I fully expect my world to be shaken upside-down and flipped
inside-out at first. Going in enlisted, without knowing anyone
will be a challenge. However, I hope to find a comfortable routine as time goes on with the exceptional deployment. As in any
career field, I know I will meet people who encourage me and
people who discourage me.

What career field did you pick and why?

I am passionate to communicate the interests of the Air Force as a Broadcast Journalist via radio and television! To explain why I chose this career field, I will briefly highlight my past five jobs. As a former Nursing Assistant, I have proven myself trustworthy to safeguard confidential information. I am strong, yet humble, and cheerfully embrace hard work. As a restaurant hostess, I am outstanding at establishing relationships with people of nearly all ages, race, and cultures. I've become proficient at record documentation as a librarian assistant. I have also learned to remain calm under pressure and time constraints as a customer service representative. My approachable demeanor and ability to ask riveting questions frequently reveal stories hidden behind the scenes. Yet, I also know the value of active listening. For these reasons and many more, I am thrilled to serve as a Broadcast Journalist.

What do you think will be the hardest part of military life?

I think the hardest part of military life will be adjusting to a government-directed schedule. I am used to having a lot of flexibility in my day and making my own decisions about where to spend my time. Constantly being told what to do and where to go makes me feel slightly awkward and less independent as an individual. However, I recognize that following directions allows me to be highly effective as a member of the service.

What are you doing to prepare to attend boot camp?

To prepare for Basic Military Training (BMT), I have worked out regularly, eaten far more protein than usual, practiced my reporting statement, asked my recruiter many questions, and joined discussion boards on Facebook. I do not intend to be shell-shocked by the rigors of BMT.

Are you worried about any part of military life?

I am concerned about how the military will impact my finances and relationships. Primarily, my savings and my boyfriend.

Being financially secure is extremely important to me, as I come from a large family and understand the costs of living. Moreover, I am anxious that the challenges of a long-distance relationship will separate me from my boyfriend. I am uncertain of our definite future, but hopeful that we have what it takes to make it through my four-year contract.

What is one thing you hope to accomplish while serving in the military?

One thing I hope to accomplish while serving in the military is international travel. Up until now, I have only ever been to six states (four of which are in the South). I believe that by seeing more of the world, I will learn to communicate more efficiently with people of other cultures and better understand what I can do to serve them.

Who do you admire and why?

I greatly admire a little-known American sculptor named Anna Ladd. She used her art to construct lifelike masks for facially mutilated French soldiers. Using an original formula, she created attractive, affordable, and reliable prosthetics for these wounded warriors. In fact, her artificial faces saved many of these men from committing suicide. Furthermore, she did all this work voluntarily, seeing it as an opportunity to model, "a Christ that shows the triumph of spirit over suffering" (El-Hai, 2005). I can relate to this Ladd because I am also an artist and love to help others with the talents God has given me.

References

El-Hai, J. (2005, July). Anna Ladd's Masks: Mending WWI's Scars. The History Channel, 3, 26-31.

AIR FORCE

*A*manda Huffman served in the United States Air Force for six years. She worked as a Civil Engineer and left the military as a Captain (O-3). She left the military when her oldest son was born and transitioned to be a stay at home mom. She is now a mom, military spouse and own Airman to Mom LLC.

Why did you decide to join the military?

September 11th and I had a lot of friends my freshman year in college either joining the military or looking into it so I decided to check it out as well. I was most interested in getting college paid for and it was my main motivator to start looking at Enlisting in the Air National Guard.

You served as an officer; how did you go from looking into enlisting to commissioning?

I was going to enlist into the Air National Guard, but a friend of mine took me to lunch and told me about the program he was doing, Reserve Officer Training Corps (ROTC). A program where I could continue going to college and then commissioned into the military sounded interesting. I went to the open house the Spring of my Freshman year of college and joined ROTC my Sophomore year while still attending community college. When I transferred to the four-year university, I got a ROTC scholarship and was able to get the last three years of my college paid for by the military.

What was your career field and what did you do?

My degree in college was Civil Engineering so I chose that career field. I did not realize how much work the Civil Engineer Squadron did for the base. They keep it running. All the way from unclogging toilets to creating and managing contracts for engineering projects on base. I worked in the Environmental Section,

Engineering Office at my first assignment at Holloman Air Force Base (AFB). I also deployed with the Army as part of a Provincial Reconstruction Team (PRT) to Kapisa, Afghanistan. My last job was at Wright-Patterson AFB where worked at Air Force Material Command doing Energy Management.

What was the neatest part of your first job in the Air Force?

The F-22 was coming to Holloman AFB when I worked in the Engineering shop and there were so many cool projects going on. Once I was helping "supervise" runway repair and the German Tornado was landing over our heads. It was the coolest thing to be out working and having airplanes landing right over your head. It was a no picture zone and cell phones were not like what we have today so I only have the memory in my mind, but I won't ever forget it.

What was your PRT deployment's mission?

Our team was supposed to help connect the Government of the Islamic Republic of Afghanistan (GIRoA) with the people. Our construction projects (roads, bridges, schools, government buildings, etc.) were nominated by the government, built by the government of Kapisa and managed by the PRT.

What was your job while deployed?

I was a Civil Engineer and that meant we were in charge of all the construction projects within Kapisa Province. When we started the deployment we were managing 26 projects ranging from flood protection to buildings to roads. We also had to run missions off the base and into Kapisa so that we could inspect (Quality Assess/Quality Control) the projects. We were also required to meet with various contractors and coordinate with other sections of the PRT.

What cultural differences do you remember between

Afghanistan and the United States?

Their down day was Friday and not Sunday. Our commander didn't understand this cultural difference and made our down day to be Sunday. It made for two days a week we couldn't really do meeting or run missions.

You also rarely saw women when we went off base for our missions. The only Afghan women I talked to were a handful of women at a women's shelter and the head of the Women of Interior in Kapisa. Women often had a burqa (a cloth covering that covers you from head to toe) or were working in the fields with their heads covered.

We had a chance to interact with the kids when we went on our missions. They had an excitement for learning and loved to talk about John Cena and always asked for pens and stickers.

What landscape differences do you remember between Afghanistan and the United States?

It was very mountainous. The terrain was very similar at the Forward Operating Base as it was in Alamogordo New Mexico. There was a lot of farming and agriculture in Kapisa. It was similar to where I grew up in California, but also very different since it was rural and small towns. There were no major freeways, barely any roads that our team could use to drive throughout the country. It was also very green the farther in the mountain you went.

Were there any particular foods that you ate while in Afghanistan that was different from the United States?

We would have something similar to kabobs from the local market (normally goat) wrapped in nan (afghan bread). It was super yummy, but you would have to watch for bones and other things in the meat. One day a contractor brought up food and he told us he had slaughtered the goat in the morning. A little different than back home.

The Afghan food was really yummy. I also remember rice with carrots and raisins and they had nuts covered in sugar that were so yummy.

What was the hardest thing you faced with the cultural difference in Afghanistan?

We spent a lot of time training for how to interact with the locals since I deployed as a Civil Engineer and my counterpart was also a female. But when we arrived in country, we were told not to wear head covering because then the contractors would look down on us.

Afghan contractor had been used to working with American women and from what I could tell they didn't seem to have a problem working with us. They might tell us that we were lazy or broken due to cultural differences, but I guess it didn't really bother me. One contractor talked about his 20 children and my friend and I were taken aback by so many kids. And when he found out American families typically have 1-3 children, he stated American women are lazy.

As a female, do you remember being treated differently because of your sex?

I guess I touched on that a little above, but I would say with the Afghans I really didn't feel like I was treated different. There were a few issues with members on our team, but I would guess those more had to do with dynamics related to things outside of gender.

Being deployed requires you to live with the people you work with and there isn't anywhere to go to get away from the people you are working with, especially on the FOB we were at.

Our team became a family. We had some people who fit into the crazy cousin that like to stir up trouble, but overall, we were a tight knit group and looked out for each other.

What challenges did you face?

Our commander wasn't the best leader. The team I was on was a mix of Army and Air Force personnel. The commander was Air Force, but being out on the ground doing tactical missions was not his expertise. It ended up that he brought down morale and it took a long time for leadership at higher levels to make changes.

By the time he was fired the deployment was almost over and we were all just ready to go home. Outsiders looking in said things that were untrue and hurt morale even more. It was a really hard deployment.

Did you have any regular frustrating situations or a

frustrating situation you can share about?

One of the things we had trouble with was helping the Afghans understand timelines and maintaining the building being handed over to them.

When we would ask for timelines, they would give completion dates that were not realistic and it made it hard for us to plan for new projects.

When projects were completed the Afghans wouldn't know how to maintain the new buildings and they would slowly fall into disrepair. We didn't have the tools needed to address the issue of building maintenance and the Afghans didn't understand what was needed because there really was no way to explain it. It was an issue throughout Afghanistan.

What is the one thing you remember most

from your deployment?

The people I met. I have three friends I still talk with regularly from the deployment. And we often say that all the bad stuff we had to deal with was worth the friendship we have today. Our

Amanda Huffman

lives have changed so much since we left Afghanistan in 2010, but we still try to get together and our friendship continues.

The friends I made that only lasted through the deployment hold a special place in my heart as well. I'm still connect with many of them through Facebook and social media.

Is there a memory or story from your deployment

you want to share?

I think the most memorable moment was when our convoy was attacked when we went to inspect a school. The next team's commander was visiting so he was on that mission. They had made a big deal about all the different sites we would take him to. But at the first project when we were about half way from the trucks and the school we were attacked.

We were lucky no one was hurt or killed, just a little rattled. We had been in Afghanistan for five months and had not been bothered by enemy forces and even though we knew there was Taliban nearby they had never attacked us. They could have easily surprised us and maybe that was their plan, but we luckily had changed our route and instead of going up to Nijrab and then hitting the school as our last stop, it was our first stop. Their attack was unorganized and we were able to get back to the vehicles quickly. This one change could have saved the lives of members on our team.

What question do you get when people find out you deployed?

You don't look like someone who was in the military. People tell me that when they find out I was in the service. And if I get a chance to tell them about my deployment they often say why. But sadly, people often don't ask me about my experience. That is why I'm writing this book.

How did you meet your husband?

My husband and I met while we were both completing the Reserve Officer Training Corps (ROTC) program at California State University, Fresno. My husband is a year a head of me and had started ROTC right after high school so when I started, he had already attended the summer boot camp program called Field Training.

We met a few times, but we didn't start dating until after we went to Lawrence Livermore National Laboratory and I got a change to know him. We did not start dating until about a month later when we both ended up on an Army ROTC trip where we were the "bad guys" for the Army cadets. It was the worst and best trip and I was happy to have joined the Air Force. Of course, not knowing one day I would deploy with the Army.

We got married my senior year of college. He had already commissioned and was living in New Mexico. When I graduated and commissioned, I followed him to New Mexico as we were lucky enough to be stationed together.

What was it like to be married to someone serving in the military?

It was complicated. We never moved at the same time. Part of it was due to choices we made that caused us to move at different times. But we were also trying to work two careers and get us to the place we needed to go next. I ended up deploying and he ended up moving to Ohio before I returned home.

Another thing that made things challenging was how hard it was for us to be stationed at the same location. It took a lot of working with leadership to get assignments at the same place. It made it hard to continue serving when we started our family. And after being separated for a year deployment I didn't know if I wanted to leave my child behind.

Is that why you left the military?

The deployment experience was a huge factor in why I left the military. I might have tried to make it work for at least a little bit. But to be honest, I didn't enjoy my job at Air Force Materiel Command Headquarters and also didn't realize what the military meant to me until after it was gone. We wrote out a list of reasons to leave or stay and in the end, it made the most sense for me to leave the military.

Luckily a few of the biggest factors have changed. Deploying six months after your child is born has been changed to 1 year and maternity leave has been changed to three months instead of six weeks. I am not sure if I would have stayed in, but it would have been a different conversation. But in the end, I am happy I left the military to be a military spouse and mom.

What would you tell women joining the military?

I would tell them to do it. If there is a desire in your heart to serve your country, don't let anything stop you. You will never regret joining the military. It will be hard. You will do things that you never would expect to do. But you will grow and learn so much about yourself. In the end, the hard parts are worth it.

J ackie* currently serving on active duty in the United States Air Force as a Major (O-4). She is an Aircraft Maintenance Officer and the Director of Operations. She has deployed to multiple locations around the world.

Why did you decide to join the military?

To travel the world and for a college scholarship.

Where have you deployed to?

Qatar

Kuwait

Syria

United Arab Emirates (UAE)

Korea

Philippines

Diego Garcia

Guam

What was you or your team's mission for your various deployments?

Most maintenance missions are inherently the same: Be able to meet your war-time commitments (this is being able to generate/produce X number of aircraft in X number of hours to do its mission).

My job at varying levels has always been to enforce training, maintenance discipline (keeping the wrench-turning legal), creating the schedule, finding the right people to do the job.

In Syria, I was the senior airfield authority for the country's key logistics hub for all DoD and also the only C-17 capable airfield. Our mission was to keep the dirt landing zone open, including performing airfield maintenance and issuing landing approvals.

What was your job while deployed?

For all of my deployments except Syria, I served in some capacity Maintenance flight line leadership. Everything from Aircraft Maintenance Unit Officer-in-Charge to Director of Operations.

These duties include scheduling and de-conflicting flight line operations/aircraft, ensure maintenance gets prioritized and completed for upcoming flights, enforcing maintenance discipline in accordance with Air Force Instructions (AFIs), dealing with people problems that arise at work (or from home), coordinating/collaborating with contractors, tracking down/ordering parts, and updating/informing/fighting with flying squadron leadership over the flying schedule.

What cultural differences do you remember between the country you went to and the United States?

I had the opportunity to travel off base in Syria, Qatar, and UAE. I was told to wear loose-fitting clothing, not engage men directly, and not show too much skin.

My only actual engagements with locals was in Syria, where key leadership exchanges took place. I had to have a senior enlisted male or male officer open up conversations before I was allowed to freely engage with my male counterparts. Although I felt that the Syrians were rather progressive in their views towards women, I was told it would be too forward to engage them directly without being "led" by my male teammates.

Did you face any challenges while you were deployed?

As mentioned above, there were cultural considerations in the

Middle East.

In the Philippines (PI) in particular, I was attached to a special operations unit that had a long history (previous base) in Angeles City, PI. We were "well-known" there for our grand expenditures and had little restrictions from frequenting bars and clubs. To be frank, a significant portion of my team (usually about 100 members, 95% male) would patron go-go clubs, strip clubs, and brothels there. It was a widely known secret.

One trip, our flight doctor was caught with a prostitute, stood trial, and was subsequently discharged and divorced from his wife. This behavior was widespread and among all ranks. The human trafficking problem there was absolutely disgusting, and we were contributing to the problem.

After three trips there (and by that time the resident PI Maintenance expert), I asked my male Commander if I could be removed from further PI trips. He agreed.

What is your favorite memory from your deployment experience(s)?

My top three:

Philippines: I was on the ground a week before an exercise we were prepping for when a super-typhoon struck the south PI. We were the first Department of Defense Logistics Element on the ground and converted our training missions into humanitarian aide and disaster relief missions.

I actually got the chance to crew a flight down into the destruction zone, fill up the cargo hold with displaced persons, and fly them into Manila to start new lives. It was both difficult to witness the loss they had experienced but rewarding to give them a new chance at building their lives back.

Syria: This was the first time in my career that I have worked outside of maintenance. Very few Airmen will ever get to say that they opened up and worked a Forward Operating Base equipped with a dirt landing strip.

I just finished up almost eight months out there in the middle of nowhere Syria surrounded by a village that was once considered an Islamic State of Iraq and Syria (ISIS) stronghold. With little airfield management knowledge, my team and I kept that airfield open and running so we could bring supplies indirectly to the warfighter.

It's the only time in my career where I could actually "see" the direct connection be my work and the relationship to the frontline. We unloaded directly from the aircraft to flatbeds that were convoying the supplies -- pretty cool!

Australia: Following a three of four tire blowout on a C-130, I lead a small team of thirteen people to the middle of Australia to change the tires, tow the aircraft (which was blocking Northern Australia's only divert airfield for military and commercial aircraft) and fix/safe the plane enough to fly it back to Japan for permanent repair. We camped out in the cargo hold and worked around the clock for ten days fixing it.

What sort of struggles have you faced? What types of struggles have you faced because you were a female serving in the Air Force?

My biggest overall struggle: I work in what has been labeled a "male-dominated" career field. If I want to follow the rules, I'm a called unflattering names. If I have an opinion you disagree with, I am called to pushy or complain too much. If I'm assertive, I have been labeled in negative words and phrases. I have the need to constantly prove my worth, no not be "too sensitive," smile more...all because I'm a woman. I have even heard people say, "I must be on my period" If I am unable to give you that extra plane you requested."

I have been sexually harassed by my Maintainers, flying squadron members, a Squadron Commander, and my own First Sergeant once. Thankfully, as I've gotten more senior in rank, I've either learned how to address this appropriately OR they are just scared of me now or maybe a little bit of both.

It really does suck though to know that my fellow sisters have to put up with this crap because I can't think of a time when my male counterparts have had to deal with this.

On the flipside, I've worked with some really awesome people, both officer and enlisted that have witnessed this and squashed it immediately.

How did being in the military affect you as a person? Did it change you? Did you learn anything about yourself?

I learned that I had to balance constantly being on guard with "proving" myself.

What would you tell women who are considering joining the military?

Follow your heart, pursue your goals. When your heart is no longer in it, change course.

What is your favorite memory from your military experience?

The small team dynamics while working humanitarian missions in the Pacific; the forced family...truly loved it!

If you are married, did your spouse serve while you were in/is he serving now?

My husband and I have both been serving on active duty for eight years.

What is the hardest part of being married to someone in the military while serving yourself (commonly called mil-to-mil)? Do you feel like you have support from the military community as a mil to mil family?

I have absolutely chosen a career over family...even though I still want a kid. Unlike my husband, I could not work in maintenance while pregnant, so I chose not to get pregnant. Being in different career fields (he's a pilot), we've spent a ton of time apart. You learn to deal with it because unlike having a civilian spouse, I understand and appreciate the feelings of excitement of deployment and going Temporary Duty (TDY) Assignment (TDY is how military members describe military business trip it could be for training, meetings, conferences, etc.) with your team. I totally get it.

It's the biggest reason we are both going Reserve though. We are tired of the lack of predictability and time apart. I was on the command list this summer and his career field doesn't progress like mine...it would have meant an assignment apart.

My husband flies E-3s and though a large community, they only have three base choices. When we were in Japan, I joined his "wives' club. I had a blast and met some great friends. I knew that coming back to Tinker Air Force Base in Oklahoma for a second time, we would be stationed with these people again. They are really great and rally together when you need them... or don't. I didn't experience this support my first time at Tinker, but I'm glad I met these ladies overseas where all we had each other. Stateside just has a slightly different vibe.

My first assignment here, my neighbors (all civilian) were REALLY awesome and helped me out while my husband was away. I don't think this is necessarily a common experience though. I find that many families are too proud to ask for help or that our civilian counterparts don't understand the military struggle and maybe feel like they are prying if they offer to help. I guess it's just personality-dependent.

A manda R is currently serving on active duty in the United States Air Force as a Captain. She attended the US Air Force Academy and commissioned into the Air Force as an Acquisitions Officer but ended up doing a tour in Space Operations. She is currently back in the Acquisitions career field, but her mission is tied to Space.

Why did you decide to join the military?

I wanted a challenge of going to the US Air Force Academy, and stayed in because I am both contributing to what I believe is a greater good that is bigger than myself and because it is hard to find an "integrity first, service before self, and excellence in all we do" mentality elsewhere.

What was the hardest part of the Academy?

I'll admit four years at the Academy is rough - academically, mentally, emotionally, physically - but that is also the (retrospective!) beauty of it. You grow stronger in so many ways, but also transition from an individual to a part of a team...you have to acknowledge that your success is built upon and fortified by the success of those around you.

Personally, I struggled with "techie" classes; I have always detested math and the core curriculum is packed with physics, astronautical and aeronautical engineering, statistics, and calculus. But I pulled through thanks to the faculty who had open doors and offered extra instruction and to my classmates who helped me study. I'd like to think I paid them back with proofreading, history, and language help!

Have you deployed?

I deployed in the summer of 2017, and it was one of the highlights of my career thus far. I was able to support the Resolute Support mission via my work as an Operational Flight Controller at NATO – SHAPE, and it was an amazing experience to get to work in another organization and alongside a number of our foreign military allies. With this experience, I am excited to see where my career takes me. I have always had high aspirations and goals; so far, the Air Force has helped me see some to fruition, like getting my Master's degree and going on language immersions to Costa Rica, Uruguay, Spain, and one upcoming to Chile! I can't wait to see what the rest of my journey in the military will have to offer.

What are you most excited about?

One of my career goals is to work in the US European Command (EUCOM), US Southern Command (SOUTHCOM, South America), and US African Command (AFRICOM) to get to utilize and build my Spanish and French languages while contributing to larger efforts with our allies to build a more secure and free world. I hope to get to work again with the North Atlantic Treaty Organization (NATO) and foreign military forces, and one day work closer with International efforts in diplomacy. Overall, working to create a more secure world and seeing the positive effect my work has, often without ever being known, is really rewarding.

What was your career field/job?

I had a unique journey to where I am today. I earned a slot as an Acquisitions Officer from the Air Force Academy but ended up doing an "operational experience" tour in Space Operations. Following that assignment, I returned to my original core as an Acquisitions Officer and now help provide today's warfighter with the equipment and systems they need to complete the mission. I got lucky to work in the office as a Program Manager for the same system I operated while in Space, which allows me to bring a unique perspective to the table as a former user who understands the mission.

Did you face any struggles while serving in the military?

Everyone has struggles regardless of their career choice, and the military is no different. It can be anything from general work frustrations to being TDY (military work trip) and away from your family. I have had to navigate being separated from my husband for a long period of time. We spent our whole first year of marriage on separate coasts of the US having to manage to pay for his full-time tuition and two separate rental and living expenses. Definitely learned good budgeting practices that year!

I have also missed the ability to be with family during important life events, such as the passing of my Great Aunt, who was like a grandma to me. Due to that experience, I will always take care of my Airmen because family truly does come first and is the bedrock for a strong career. In fact, I recently turned down selection to my dream assignment because it would not support my family's future. It was an extremely painful situation to go through, but again, family first.

Overall, these struggles were really unique to me and my story, but I've found everyone eventually faces their own distinct hard times...the best we can do with them is get up a little stronger, find the pony in the room, and remember it later when we can turn around and offer a hand to someone else in need.

If you faced any difficulties did any of your struggles directly relate to the fact you are a female?

Unfortunately, women endure hardships regardless of the sector they work in, as is truly coming to light in the #MeToo movement. I don't think any "difficulties" have arisen because of my gender, although I have dealt with a bit of pettiness...like when I had an old Academy grad say the Academy was a better place before women or when I was asked to clean and decorate for a luncheon because "you women do it better."

Sometimes, in society in general, I feel the female airman is not often thought about. Like when a restaurant has a military discount and the waiter instinctively thanks my husband for his service or the instance when an airline doing active military pre-boarding demand to see my ID...but they didn't ask for an ID for the two men in front of me who were also not in uniform. Women in service are just not very prevalent in the public eye and therefore just naturally aren't the first thing someone thinks of when they hear "Airman." At work, I would like to say, the vast majority of my male counterparts are professionals who I am fortunate to get to serve beside. What is truly refreshing is more recently having men try to understand the female perspective. The best way to make a change is with dialogue and I think the military is taking a great turn to have such necessary discussions.

How did being in the military affect you as a person? Did it change you? Did you learn anything about yourself?

I'm not sure I have changed much because I feel like the same person. I would say that the military has allowed me many new experiences, introduced me to both different people and thoughts and different experiences and trials that continuously shape me as a person little by little.

What would you tell women who are considering joining the military?

Do it. Do what you want to do. Don't let the fear of the unknown hold you back. Don't let scared rhetoric or bad experiences of others stop you from pursuing your dreams, no matter what they are. The military itself is not any more dangerous than the rest of society or other large organization. Probably much less so because of the standards of conduct and discipline. Of course, go in with open eyes and ears and stand up for yourself and others when the time comes to do so. Seek out a mentor, a female mentor, who has gone before you and is someone you can turn to when life gets hard or circumstances get rough...but these words are ones I would share with any young woman, regardless of her intended profession.

What is your favorite memory from your military experience?

Wow. There are so many. Jumping out of a plane five times and getting my jump wings, shaking President Obama's hand at graduation and traveling to different countries for language immersions. Those are the big ones, but little things occur as well that tend to get lost in the memory of time...from the satisfaction of getting a program to the next milestone, to doing well in a training course or earning an award, to just random goofiness and interaction with my friends, to coming home after a long trip and finally getting to hug my husband. Military life is challenging, but also, for me, has been so rewarding.

*B*onnie Reeves served on active duty in the United States Air Force. She reached the rank of Master Sergeant (E-7). She worked in Logistics Supply, working on various jobs in supply support ranging from aircraft to vehicles to communications. She met her husband while serving on active duty and they have now both retired from the military. During her career, she faced multiple deployments and even faced the challenge of being deployed at the same time as her husband. While leaving her children in the care of her Mother-in-Law. Read the amazing story of the challenges of dual military life.

Why did you decide to join the military?

To serve my country and travel

Where did you deploy to?

South America, Kuwait, Germany

What was your job while you were deployed?

My job always revolves around supply. I either worked a supply or logistics squadron or I was out in the squadron like Transportation or an Aircraft Squadron. I basically provide support by parts needed to fix items from computers to Aircraft. Anything in-between. Along with the items like toilet paper to uniforms items needed for the region we were in.

What deployment was the most memorable and why?

Some deployments were more like a vacation. I deployed to South America to Curacao. It is an island that actually belonged to the Netherlands. Anyway, it was a paradise. I was there for 60 days spent most of my time in a bathing suit. It was a twelve-man team I was a Supply troop the rest were Maintenance and we had one aircraft we supported.

We had to be there when it took off and landed. Fix it when broke and not wear our uniforms till we were at the airport where it was parked. We stayed in a five-star hotel on the beach. It was awesome. It really beat the ones where you're in the desert and heat with no water.

This was before children I was 29 and still, in good shape, it was just a great time except that my husband was not with me. I had a great group of guys that knew my husband and treated me with respect and protected me if needed. I knew nothing was going to happen with my eleven big brothers.

What was the hardest part of being deployed?

Separation from my family and know if I were to screw up at times it really could be someone's life on the line.

Did you experience any differences between the culture of the US and the various countries you visited?

In Saudi and Riyadh, you are considered as a woman a second-class citizen there. I had to wear headgear when we went out and going to and from work. Walking six paces from your male escort and the fact that the male escorts were not your husbands you just really had to not draw attention to yourself. Scary.

What is your favorite memory(ies) from your deployment experiences?

Before our children were born my husband and I got to deploy to Germany together. They arranged for us to get adjoining rooms that share a bathroom in the barracks we stayed in, so we were able to spend some time together and travel. Not a lot of time but we were very thankful for the time we had because we could have been separated.

He works Mid-shift Monday through Friday which is 2300 –

0700. While I worked three on three off twelve-hour shifts 0700 to 1900. We went to Paris and a few other trips and brought back lots of sweet wine. It was a great hooray before children.

Did you face any challenges deployed because you were a female?

I think now that I am out in the civilian world, we are probably more advanced in this area in the enlisted ranks than civilian companies in certain career fields. I would run across a person now and then that did not like someone in charge as a woman but there was not a lot, they could do about it.

If you faced any difficulties did any of your struggles directly relate to the fact you are a female?

A few problems with troops not wanting a woman in charge.

How were you able to overcome this challenge?

There are standards put in place to address them paperwork and protocol. You just follow the rulebook and if you do it right, you're covered. It still doesn't feel good, but hey.

How did being in the military affect you as a person? Did it change you? Did you learn anything about yourself?

Showed me I could do anything I could put my mind to and even then, some. You have to rely on others as a team

How did you meet your husband?

We met in a training class when stationed at Little Rock AFB, AR

How did your life change when you married your spouse?

Um, I really was carefree and did what I wanted when I wanted to take lots of deployments for married people because at the time we could exchange and not have to go like the system works now. This is my second marriage. My first was a little different. We really never lived together because of the military and that is why we grew apart. We were really good friends and made the mistake of marrying in the first place.

What was it like to be a dual military couple?

Good and bad. The money was good and we both were dedicated to our work. The understanding of what we had to do at times helped when both of us were active duty. Getting the same time off together or going to double function sometimes got old. At times there was the 'whose job is more important' struggle.

What challenges did you face while both serving in the military?

The biggest challenge would be our children and making sure they were taken care of and they knew we always look out for them whether we physically were there not. Working late, getting dinner on the table, making them feel just as important as our work was our goal.

What challenges did you face as a mil-mil family during deployments?

When one of us is gone we still have the hard work at our jobs plus the home stuff. In the military, you have more awareness of what is really happening because of classified briefings, work around the shop and having deployed before. It is different than if you are military spouse and don't know what your spouse is doing. Sometimes it can be good thing and other times it is scary.

What is the hardest part of being a mom while serving overseas?

Leaving your babies.

How do you stay connected with your child(ren) while being deployed?

When I deployed it was before Skype and Facetime and they were smaller and really couldn't read or write just yet so we mostly did what little phone conversation we could, and pictures sent by email.

Did you face any challenges with your spouse being deployed while serving on active duty?

When 9/11 happened, I was three months pregnant with our oldest. I knew I was not going to deploy but knew my husband would. About three weeks after he left and when he arrived at his location, they told him he was forward deploying and that where he was going was not even bare base, they were one of the first teams in country.

They were told to warn spouses that they were not going to have communication or mail for at least thirty days but to prepare for sixty. It was not what you wanted to hear when you're pregnant with your first child and hope your husband gets back in time for the birth. It was a rough deployment.

By far his worst deployment mentally and physically, he had some close calls and was changed when he returned. I think our child was a lifesaver in his life and our marriage just because we had something to focus on. He got back a week before Trevor was born, I was in thirty hours of labor, and Michael slept on the floor and held my hand and never left my side. He did have to leave three months after Trevor was born. I think that was a hard one on both of us as well.

What would be one piece of advice you would give to others facing deployment when their spouse is serving?

Communication. There is nothing that will get you through better. Have it before you leave during and when you get back. I think if we stress anything to our kids it is, "always communicate." Either both deployed or one person deploying? The same and realize what you want and what you get might be two different things but know that the other person is doing every-thing they can to give you what they can. Sometimes, Uncle Sam just does not see it your way. Be understanding and patient.

What is the hardest part of being a dual military couple?

When our boys were three and eighteen months, we both had to deploy and leave them to my husband's mother to care for them. We (Michael and I) were apart for nine months that year and three of those months our children were with her.

We will never get that time back.

It really lets you know the difference between knowing with-out a doubt your children are cared for with your spouse to hav-ing someone, not us taking care of them. She was their Grand-mother, but it just wasn't the same. He was in Al Udeid. I was in Kuwait. Right before he left to go home his Chief told him to go pack an overnight bag and be back in an hour when he got off shift. The Chief knew I was deployed too and that we would not see each other for another four months.

Michael being the person he was didn't really as any questions. He just went and packed a bag. When he returned, he said, "Call your wife tell her you are you will be on the ground for four hours to visit with her, pack an overnight bag just in case the plane breaks." He said it was the least he could do.

He did not call me he called my boss to let them know so he could surprise me. I was the Vice President of the five to six club over there and we were putting on a fun run so my boss told him where I was and let someone there know not to let me leave. The run was along the flight line, so he didn't have far to get to me. I am sitting there at the check-in table and I see a guy walk-ing my way with his uniform on and I say to the person next to me, "If I didn't know better, I would say the guy coming this way is my husband he walks just like him." As he gets closer, he smiles and well let's just say I knew then it was him.

We went and got coffee and just sat and had longer than a ten-minute phone conversation for the next 4 hours. I can't tell you what we talked about because that wasn't the point it was just that we got to be in each other's presence for a little while in the middle of our crazy!

I had to leave my youngest on the day after he turned six months for my deployment. He became a Daddy's boy and I never got him back. It hurt.

How did you overcome the challenges of military life to both make it to retirement?

God, communication, understanding, love, support from your military family, mentors in front of us that did it as well and knowing that there was an end of the tunnel. I think you either have the resilience to withstand what the military puts you through or you don't. Knowing we had each other's back when we were away and that nothing changed as far as that support no matter what.

What is the best benefit of both being retired from the military?

Our ability to both retire and spend time with our children before they leave the nest. We had our children late in our military careers and sometimes that is a good thing and sometimes bad. You go through the stage of the sick kid who is going to take off whose job is more important to take off and then the deployments and missing the important parts of their lives because you're gone.

I retired when the boys were in 2nd and 4th grade. I did not work for the next five years. I volunteered in their classroom, went on every field trip and was there when it counted. We had summers together to explore and do things they could remember forever. We had a sit-down full breakfast and dinner almost every day with all of the family when Michael was not deployed, and it made a difference. If I did not retire, I would have had to work to help support the family but with my retirement coming in I didn't have to.

Michael retired the summer before the boys were 9th and 7th grade. To me, these are the years they need their Father for development and becoming a man. With both our retirements and very good planning he doesn't have to work.

I substitute for their high school for a little extra income. We don't have money to spend willy-nilly, but we are surviving and have a wonderful place to spend our retirement. We provide for the boys and they finally have a place to come back to. I am 47 and Michael is 41 so we have plenty of youth left in us. But we can make every sports game, and every art event. We can be there when they need us, and nothing stands in our way. It is a wonderful feeling from not able to make vacation plans because you don't know rather you are going to be deployed or not.

What is your favorite memory from your military experience?

While stationed at Abilene I had a team of Airmen that you could say was my ride or die team. We had each other's back and there was never a question of loyalty to each other or the job. We worked hard and played hard most of the time shorthanded.

What would you tell women who are considering joining the military?

They can do it. Find a few good friends to lean on when times get rough and do be afraid to stand up for what's right.

C *ynthia Cline is currently serving as a Captain in the United States Air Force alongside her husband. Right after her daughter's first birthday, she was required to deploy, spending the next six months in Turkey. This is where she was inspired to start her blog, A Faithful Step. Her story is one of overcoming challenges and becoming stronger through all of it. She is a Force Support Officer and works in the Personnel career field.*

Why did you decide to join the military?

Long story short, my father is a veteran of the United States Air Force. My father was my hero growing up, so joining the Reserve Officer Training Corp (ROTC) was a way for me to honor him. I joined ROTC to learn more about the Air Force not realizing what ROTC actually encompassed. I initially joined for my father, but stayed in for the community.

What are the duties of your job overall?

Personnel is a vast career field. A simple way to think about a Force Support Officer is to think of the term "cradle to grave". The Force Support Squadron essentially provides all the support to a base. We maintain the Child Development Centers (cradle) through Mortuary Services and Honor Guard (Grave). Some of my previous positions include:

Manpower: I studied certain functions or organizations to determine how many people (actually requirements) it would take to do a job/man a unit. For example, a manpower technician would study a person's job, then develop an equation ($y=mx+b$), which in turn would tell you how many people it would take to complete said job.

Personnel: I oversaw the passport office, dependent identifications/Common Access Cards (military identification cards), awards and decorations, assignments, retirements and separations, evaluations, and anything related to careers (over 70 different programs).

Services: I have had a little experience with overseeing a golf course, bowling alley, a few dining facilities, as well as putting on events for the community. More recently, I have started overseeing the lodging facilities and the fitness centers on base.

Readiness: The most rewarding and challenging job was readiness. I was in charge of our mortuary technicians and honor guard team. During my first nine weeks on the job, I assisted with nine Active Duty cases. Of these cases, one member was a member from my squadron; another was someone I used to work with and had a great working relationship with. I was even given the honor of presenting an American flag to a grieving mother of a veteran who committed suicide.

Again, cradle to grave support.

Did you face any struggles while serving in the military?

From the very beginning I have struggled with a variety of things. In ROTC, I struggled with fitness. To give you an idea of how out-of-shape I was, my first day at PT (physical training), I was unable to continuously run for 200 meters. I would barely make it down a straight a way of the track before stopping in complete exhaustion. It took me over two years to catch up with my peers. Due to the competitive nature and comparing myself, I suffered from low self-esteem and unhealthy habits of trying to lose weight.

Do you still face challenges with meeting the Physical Fitness Test requirements?

Unfortunately, yes, although not in the same way. Physical Fitness doesn't come easily to me. I have to train all year, almost five days a week in order to score above an excellent yet there are people (like my husband) who barely train and can score 90+ on a test.

Postpartum, the challenges increased. During my pregnancy, I couldn't run due to extreme pelvic pain, so I had to start as if I had never worked out in my life. Thankfully, the Air Force now allows you to test the month your baby turns one-years-old. Previously, you would have to test about six months post-partum and I am not sure I would have passed.

Did you face any other struggles in the military?

In my second unit, I had to work with an extremely toxic commander who drove three of my members to enroll in Mental Health.

What about the commander made the environment so difficult?

This commander had no empathy, did not care about his individuals, and expected everyone to work at all hours of the day regardless of how it affected them personally. He micromanaged every single task, talked down to people, and expected everyone to work long hours and weekends in an extremely emotionally charged job (mortuary) without any time to mentally process everything.

A specific example – I had a member come back from deployment and she was on her two weeks of rest and recuperation (R&R). She was a single mom of two little girls. Due to a mortuary case, he made me call her into work and she was never given that time off. We had other people who could have helped with the case, but instead, he wanted this specific woman. There was a time where I picked up her daughters and watched them so that she could go into work. At no point did the commander ever thank her for working hard. Nor did he ever giver her time back. On multiple occasions, he also threw us under the bus for the sake of his own career.

Eventually, everyone sought mental health assistance, although I believe it could have been avoided had we had a non-toxic leader taking care of us.

It is great you were able to support your troops by getting them connected with mental health resources. Did you have to overcome a negative mental health stigma?

Surprisingly no. Everyone realized it was necessary. One of my members needed help because work had created problems with their marriage. Another was struggling with having to inspect the body of one of her coworkers. Thankfully, they all realized this was essential. I am a huge proponent for mental health (I have my Masters in Human Services Counseling: Military Resilience).

Were the people who went to mental health able to get the help they needed?

Thankfully yes, but I don't think you ever really get over some of the difficulties this commander put us through and the challenges of working mortuary.

If you faced any difficulties did any of your struggles directly relate to the fact you are a female?

There were times where I had to assert my authority as an officer over male SNCO's and civilians who did not like working for a young woman. To date – my hardest struggle has been working with other women both higher and lower ranking. For example, I tried to connect with some of my enlisted ladies and somehow got dragged into some "he said, she said" drama. As for higher-ranking female officers, I have found that I need to work harder to "impress" them than their male counterparts.

Most recently, being a mom and having to leave my daughter behind has significantly impacted me. Not saying my husband did not have it hard leaving our daughter behind for his deployment, but there is a difference when mom deploys versus dad, both for the service members and the kid(s).

During the time of this interview you are currently deployed to Turkey, what is the hardest part of being a mom while serving overseas?

The hardest part changes every day. Some days, the hardest part is seeing her little face on the phone playing with her toys and wishing I could play with her. Or having to watch my husband do most of the parenting and not have a say (Who am I to judge my husband for his dinner choices when I'm not there to help him).

Other days, the hardest part is knowing other women are interacting with her. My friends who get to have her over for playdates. Genuinely helping our family out, yet I get jealous of their interaction.

Most times, the hardest part is seeing a different baby on that screen; one with more teeth and more hair who talks a lot more and runs all over the house. I have missed those little moments I will never get back.

How do you stay connected with your child while being deployed?

Thankfully communication works really well. I purchased a data plan that gives me 50 GB a month. I can video chat during bath times and the hubby sends me a few photos. I currently have a book that I am going to record myself reading to her and send it to her soon.

Your husband is also on active duty, how did you meet your husband?

We met at The Ohio State University. We were both in the ROTC and were pledging to join a service organization called Arnold Air Society. We were in the same pledge class and became really good friends. Between sophomore and junior year, we would sometimes make out, but nothing ever came of it until senior year when we both finally admitted we had feelings for each other. The rest is history.

How did your life change when you married your spouse?

When I was single (not married), all of my decisions were self-centered. What kind of house did I want to live in? What color couch do I want? What do I want to eat for dinner? How late do I want to stay out tonight? When we got married, that all changed. It wasn't about me, me, me, but instead about us. I went from living by myself for three years, to having to pick a house with a person who had different and sometimes competing priorities. He absolutely needed a dishwasher whereas I absolutely needed an area to entertain guests. Everything finances related changed. I could no longer go out and spend hundreds of dollars on whatever I wanted. In the beginning, it felt like I had to ask for permission when in reality, it was just ensuring that we were both respectful of each other.

Have you ever had to spend time apart during your career, outside of your deployment?

Our relationship started out as long distance. When we started dating, I lived two hours away. I had graduated college and moved back with my parents until the Air Force called me to Active Duty. Then I moved to Illinois and he moved to Florida. When we got married, we were still long distance. My husband and I spent our first year of marriage apart due to Air Force assignments. Once we moved to England and lived together, we both went on multiple TDYs (military work trips/trainings), and my husband deployed when our daughter was five months old. We have actually had to spend quite a bit of time apart.

What was the hardest part of being geographically separated from your spouse?

Amanda Huffman

Two things stand out. The first is that when you need physical support, your spouse may not always be able to take leave to help you out. For example, the first year of our relationship my husband, then boyfriend, was in Florida and I moved to Illinois. During that time, he lost his grandmother unexpectedly, and I lost my grandfather and uncle. During times where we just needed a shoulder to cry on, we had to accept a phone call or text message instead.

The second was trying to figure out how to be a husband and wife when you live in different homes. How do you manage finances? Trying to figure out how to have those discussions proved challenging. Also making each other a priority. It was very easy to get busy with volunteering or hanging with friends that sometimes I would be too busy to talk on the phone. I figured I wasn't going to put my life on hold waiting for the rare occasion he could call. Instead, I was just making it more difficult for us to communicate.

Did you face any challenges with your spouse being deployed while serving on active duty?

HA! Have you heard of Murphy's law?

While my husband was gone the first time, I was five to six months pregnant, my tire popped on a small country road. I had no signal, so I was unable to reach anyone, and I had to wait for a stranger to stop and help (took about 20-30 minutes). Five days later, I was driving down the road in my husband's truck and hit a pheasant, which smashed the windshield. I had gone through two vehicles in less than a week!

On multiple occasions, my daughter had her worst nights while my husband was gone. Think projectile vomit, no sleep, etc.

On top of everything, managing how to get my daughter and myself ready to make it work on time. Juggling meetings and standard workload while pumping. Keeping up with house chores. And somehow finding the time to work out so I could pass my Physical Fitness test. Life, in general, is a challenge when you're pulling solo parent ops.

What is it like to be a dual military couple?

Surprisingly, this is a hard question. Seeing as I've only known dual military life, it's hard for me to compare our marriage with non-dual military couples. My husband and I both took the same oath yet have very different jobs. Sometimes I joke that we serve in different Air Forces. There are still lots of things we can't talk about with regards to his work and that can be extremely frustrating. Due to my background/military knowledge, I tend to ask the right/wrong questions that result in, "I can neither confirm nor deny that" response from my husband.

Financially, we are pretty secure, and it's nice to know our paychecks will be almost exactly the same amount every 1st and 15th. More recently, our work lives have started to intersect and that can make things very complicated. Luckily, we try to leave work at work and still find ways to communicate that doesn't involve the Air Force.

What challenges do you face while both serving in the military?

In the military, the mission comes first. When two people in a relationship both serve, they basically accept the fact that work will have to come first pretty often. When one person has the opportunity to put family first, the other person might not have the opportunity. There may be times when neither of us can put family first. When that's the case, consider what happens to our daughter... who puts her first?

What is the hardest part of being a dual military couple?

The hardest part of dual military life is trying to plan anything. For example, my husband is usually on a pretty set deployment cycle whereas I am not. He deployed last year and then a few months later I deployed. We had to change a lot of plans around due to my deployment, to include cancelling a few TDYs (military work trips/trainings) he had lined up.

When we try to take leave for the holidays, my husband has to contend with the flying schedule and make sure there are enough people available to fly. I, on the other hand, have to allow my subordinates to schedule their plans and then work around them. So typically, a schedule that works for my husband does not work for me. When our child gets sick the mission is impacted. We usually have to discuss which impact is greater, his or mine.

Are you planning to stay in the military for 20 years as a dual military couple? What factors will determine if this will happen?

Honestly, I don't know. Every day is different in regards to how long I will stay in the military. My husband has a longer commitment than I do, so if someone ends up leaving it will be me. Money and benefits is a huge perk to staying in. There is no hiding the fact that dual officers get paid really well, but sometimes the money isn't worth the sacrifice and stress.

Having someone else dictate when you are allowed to visit family, having to contend with two separate supervisors to try to take off the same day, having to always put the mission first is exhausting. Ultimately, my husband and I were the ones who took the oath, not our daughter. I want her to have the best life and I'm not sure that dual military parents can do that. It comes down to weighing what will be most important when we turn 80 years old. Will it be that retirement certificate and memories or will it be the family life we cultivated. That answer differs for many couples.

How did being in the military affect you as a person? Did it change you? Did you learn anything about yourself?

Being in the military did change me. I come from a Hispanic family living in inner-city Cleveland, where most people don't leave their neighborhood. Not only did I leave my neighborhood, I also left the country! I have learned that I can survive leaving a child behind to serve our country. I learned that sometimes, being a woman means you have to try a little bit harder to gain the respect of your male and female coworkers. I also learned that when push comes to shove, I can achieve anything the Air Force requires of me.

What would you tell women who are considering joining the military?

You can do it! Embrace your differences. You were created to be a woman, do not be ashamed of what that all entails. Do not force yourself to be a man just to fit in. If you have a passion for serving others, then the military is the ultimate service and your gender does not deter your ability to serve.

What is your favorite memory from your military experience?

During my last assignment, I had an extremely toxic commander. If I had been able to, I would have separated from the military just to get away from him. During my last day, I had a small going away event with my flight. One of my members created a beautiful wooden box for me. On the outside, she had a plate that said, "Whenever you are frustrated or upset, open this box and remember why you serve". Inside the box were hundreds of personalized notes from everyone in my squadron. When she presented me that box, I wept. Despite feeling like I had failed my flight, they appreciated everything I had done for them. In that moment, I realized I continue to serve to protect those I oversee. As long as I take care of my troops, then I have done my job. Receiving that gift has been the highlight of my career

*T*rish Alegre-Smith served in the United States Air Force on both active duty and in the reserves. She worked as both an Aircraft Maintenance Officer and Acquisitions Officer (Program Manager). Trish left the military as a Major (O-4) and is now a professional photographer specializing in headshots, corporate events, and visual branding.

Why did you decide to join the military?

The Air Force, through its Reserve Officer Training Corps (ROTC) scholarship program, offered the best opportunity for me to attend college and finish without debt.

Have you deployed? If yes, where?

Yes--Incirlik (Turkey) and Prince Sultan Air Base (PSAB) in Saudi Arabia in support of Operations Northern Watch, Southern Watch, and Enduring Freedom. This was during a time that many of our "long" deployments were 90 days and as young officers, we were competing to get assigned to go since there weren't slots for everyone. Very different from today's demands.

What deployment was the most memorable?

My deployment to PSAB shortly after 9/11 will always be at the forefront of my memories. The world, my perspective, and our military changed in that timeframe. I went from serving for myself (repayment for my undergraduate degree) to serving in defense of my country.

Military service and deployments after this pivotal event shaped what serving in the military would look like in the next 17+ years (e.g. multiple long-term deployments, permanent "temporary" presence in various Areas of Responsibility [AORs], deployment preparation as matter-of-fact for annual training).

This is also the deployment where my husband and I were engaged, where I faced my biggest challenges and successes in my career (at that time), and the experience that defined me as an officer.

What was the hardest part of being deployed?

The hardest part of being deployed was the fear of the unknown. I learned most of what I needed "on the job" upon arrival. I looked for experience and mentors in senior Non-Commissioned Officers (NCOs) and senior officers who were willing to "show me the ropes." I may have studied continuity from predecessors, walked around and asked questions, etc. but leading and managing the activities that came my way still involved trial-and-error on my part—and my results weren't consistent.

Did you experience any differences between the culture of the US and the various countries you visited? What were they?

I grew up in a culturally diverse area outside of Washington, D.C. and traveled to other countries so the idea of cultural differences wasn't new for me. In both Turkey and Saudi Arabia working with any host nation counterparts involved building trust on a personal level before an effective working relationship could be established. I recall meetings starting with tea and starting late was common.

Traveling to most areas in Turkey I generally dressed more modestly than I would in the U.S. at the same summer temperatures (more business casual or "Casual Friday" attire for the office) to match the locals but never felt out-of-place. The Turkish were incredibly hospitable and welcoming to visitors. At the time, we could leave the base for local shopping and restaurants as well as excursions to well-known tourist areas. This is no longer the case and the security situation is very different now.

In Saudi Arabia, only selected individuals could leave base—and women were expected to wear the black abayas (loose-fitting, full-length robes) when they did. We were briefed on how conservative the culture would be (relative to our own) but it doesn't sink in until you see it for yourself. However, what really stood out for me was to see so many labor positions (especially unskilled) filled by foreigners (known to us as Third Country Nationals or TCNs) from South and East Asian countries.

Was your job the same each time you deployed?

No, each time the position and responsibilities were different—although within what was expected of our career field. At that time, Aircraft Maintenance and Munitions were still combined for the Officer Air Force Specialty Code. On my first deployment I worked on the flight line and on the second I primarily worked in the Munitions Storage Area also known as the "bomb dump."

What is your favorite memory from the deployment?

Getting engaged while on deployment—it was the last thing that either my now-husband or I least expected to happen. We dated for less than six months and had been apart for some time when I left for deployment ahead of him. He wasn't prepared (it took a couple of months after we returned for us to get a formal engagement ring) and didn't have a plan. We met up after one of our shifts and talked about what we were planning for after our return and for the next assignments. Next thing we know, we're engaged. Both of us had that rare moment of clarity where we could see where our lives were going, and we knew it was together.

Did you face any challenges deployed because you were a female?

Yes, and I consider myself lucky as the challenges that I faced were ones I found as hurdles rather than walls. There were few other female officers or NCOs in my career field so when I did find support or mentorship from those who were successfully navigating their deployments it was great. On the flip side, I had other female officers (more senior than myself) who had attempted to mentor me but turned out to be a negative influence that I learned to distance myself from. It took some blunders and honest feedback from peers and subordinates (for which I'm still grateful) to see how their advice was misguided at best and most often wrong. I knew by reputation that these "mentors" weren't well-respected up and down their chain, but I wanted to give them a chance—because I thought they may have been unfairly judged. Looking back, I see how naïve I was then.

The most significant challenge that came my way was the first time a Staff Sergeant (E-5) challenged my authority by yelling back at me in disagreement—in public—and I froze. I didn't have the confidence in myself yet to correct him on the spot. I just stood there in shock. The senior NCO with me ended up speaking up when I did not—then he pulled me aside for a very important lesson. He pointed out what I already knew about myself: that I would need to project confidence in how I carried myself and responded to others. My short, petite frame and face that looked younger than my age (more like a teenager than an adult) did not help me so I needed to learn how to be more assertive. He warned that if I let this happen again that I would lose the respect of my Airmen and embolden others to show the same disrespect—so he advised me to not avoid this SSgt and to not show any insecurity in front of him (even if I felt it). It was difficult and terrifying for me at first, but I heeded his advice--then and now.

What sort of struggles did you face?

It was a rough adjustment coming into the military at first. Training in Air Force Reserve Officer Training Corps (AFROTC) gave me a glimpse but the first day on active duty was an eye-opener. Where I grew up, I knew and went to school with military families, but I had no one in my close family who was in the military. I didn't have a frame of reference on either the job I was going into but the culture with which I was about to become a part of.

I questioned myself a lot in the first few years—and I took every criticism to heart. There were things that I excelled at that made me stand out, but I really struggled relating and connecting to many of those who worked with me and for me—even when we were the same age. We all came from different backgrounds and had different paths in our lives. It was a huge learning curve, and humbling, for me to learn how to put myself in someone else's shoes.

I also learned how different career fields are in the Air Force—with each field having its own distinct culture, norms, and career paths. It was jarring to go from Aircraft Maintenance (where I felt like I was part of "the fight") to Acquisitions as a program manager where I felt like I was beginning a transition back into civilian life. There were more government civilians and contractors working around me than fellow Airmen—many of who were veterans with more experience than me. The entire first year I felt like an outsider--as if I were working at a different speed than my co-workers. I had to learn how to collaborate more, direct less, and adjust my own expectations.

I once had a senior officer tell me that my greatest strength was "knowing what I didn't know" and not being afraid to admit it. This made it easier for me to find mentors and allies who could steer me away from mistakes that were irrecoverable and career-killers.

What were the struggles you faced because you were a female in the military?

The primary struggles that I faced are best described in the struggles that I faced while on deployment.

How did being in the military affect you as a person? Did it

change you? Did you learn anything about yourself?

I developed skills and strength in a faster period of time than anywhere else I could imagine. College prepared me for working in the corporate world; the military prepared me for facing difficult challenges in life and succeeding. I learned that I am stronger than others had given me credit for--now I reflect that strength and confidence.

What would you tell women who are considering joining the military?

Joining the military is a worthwhile journey that can help you push past boundaries you may have set for yourself--but it is not an easy life. However, some of the best experiences in life are not easy.

What is your favorite memory from your military experience?

Taking command of my first flight of 113 airmen and the support my senior NCOs gave me (I keep in touch with many of them today thanks to social media).

If you are married, did your spouse serve while you were in/is he serving now?

Yes, and yes.

Did you face challenges as you both served in the military?

Yes—in the first years of our marriage we put a priority on our careers and that limited our time together. It took over a year before we even had the same address as we pursued a Join Spouse Assignment (a program the military has in place to help get married people stationed together). Then when we finally lived in the same house he was on frequent deployments and TDYs (military work trips/trainings) and I was on the road often as well—and our schedules didn't always match up. When our positions (and budgets) changed and travel slowed almost three years after our wedding, we finally went on our honeymoon and began the true adjustment period of learning to live with each other.

It was also assumed to never need help or support from my husband's unit since I was active duty and should have my own support system and First Sergeant in my own organization. It didn't bother me at the time since I did have a good program office to lean on. I just found this interesting as I'm no longer in uniform but still a military spouse. I also wondered what it would be like if I was assigned to a less supportive unit.

What was the hardest part of both you and your spouse being in the military?

We arrived at the point in both of our careers where it became difficult and then impossible for us to stay together as a family (the tipping point came when our second child had been born) and continue to be in the military together. We were now in two different career fields and finding positions for both of us at the same base or close in locations was looking more unlikely as we advanced in rank. I had transferred to the reserves when we were trying to start a family to give us more flexibility. That move only allowed us to flex so far.

We encountered the one assignment where childcare options were few and the waiting lists for desired options were longer than our expected time at the location. I knew that with my background and experience I had more opportunities for an easier transition to employment in the civilian world. What we weren't expecting is how difficult that transition would be for me and that it would take over four years for me to get on the path to success.

How did you and your spouse meet?

We were competing for the same job (he got the position). We did end up working together--with mutual respect coming before love.

E   *mily* is currently serving on active duty as a Captain in the United States Air Force. She has recently completed a year-long deployment to Afghanistan. She is a Logistics Officer-. As a single female officer she has faced challenges without having a support network some of her married co-workers have. She has also learned to stand up for herself and not allow men to take advantage of the fact that she is a young female.*

Why did you decide to join the military?

In all honesty, someone told me they thought I couldn't do it, and I wanted to prove them wrong, and then I took to it, surprising everyone (not least of all, myself!).

Have you deployed?

Yes, I recently returned from a year-long tour in Afghanistan.

What is you or your team's mission?

We advise the Afghan Ministry of Interior (police) on Logistics (processes, commodities, budget).

What is your job?

I advise on the creation and management of the Ministry of Interior (MoI) logistics budget, as well as the procurement, maintenance, and accountability of police weapons.

What cultural differences do you remember between Afghanistan and the United States?

Ha ha. How much time do we have? In my day-to-day, I noticed that most of my Afghan counterparts tended to go out of their way to impress me and get me what I needed, but I also worked with some who tended to brush me off. Everyone was very polite externally, however. The only issue I ever had was a general I'd never worked with glaring at me from across a table during a meeting. I was sitting behind my Afghan counterpart and whispering in his ear during a meeting, and this guy didn't seem to like that. It didn't really bother me, as I had a great relationship with my counterpart and that's all that really mattered. I also noticed that, in general, deadlines are much looser there. If the coalition needs something by Friday, we may get it by the following Thursday. We call it AST, or "Afghan Standard Time".

On a more personal side, my 23-year-old Afghan (but very Western) interpreter struggled with boundaries and what constitutes acceptable conversation between colleagues, especially men and women, but I chalked that up to him reaching maturity in a war zone while trying to navigate the oddities of a repressed culture.

Did you face any challenges while you deployed? If yes, what were they?

I had to deal with a few home issues. Not married and no kids, but I had a friend watching my dog and two other friends watching my cats. My older cat had some medical issues that required medication, and my hyper dog pulled the doggy-equivalent of his Anterior Cruciate Ligament (ACL). It was expensive, but I was more concerned about him being hurt and me not being there with him, as well as my friend who had to keep him immobile while he healed.

When I got home, I realized that moving my dog from a home he lived in for nearly two years (longer than I'd had him) was cruel, so now he lives with her permanently. It was rough, but I knew that's what was best.

Also, and I'll just be honest here, but Afghan bathrooms are GROSS. Women's restrooms tend to be even worse; I assume because women tend to be less-represented in government so they put less importance on ensuring their private spaces are sanitary.

Did you face any challenges while you have been deployed because you were a female? If yes, what were they?

I dealt with a situation where a person who worked in my 30+ person open office made inappropriate comments to me (calling me gorgeous, accusing me of giving more attention to our adopted office cat than him, etc.). I struggled with how to deal with it and just tried to ignore him while I figured out what to do. When I subconsciously started changing my routine to avoid him, I knew I had to do something. Why should *I* have to change anything about my life because this dude is being inappropriate? I promised myself that the next time he said anything, I'm firing back. The next day he called me "gorgeous", and I responded with "It's actually pronounced 'Captain'." There wasn't a problem after that, and he redeployed fairly soon after that. I was angry with myself for not doing more earlier on, but it's the standard professional woman's dilemma, i.e. "I don't want to rock the boat" and all that nonsense *eye roll*

I also had to handle Afghan men trying to get too familiar. I had to give out my email address for professional reasons, and a few times ended up with emails that were a bit too familiar. Not creepy, just... very familiar! Also, I had to put my aforementioned interpreter in his place sometimes when he made sexual comments – not ABOUT me, just in general – and explain to him that this is not acceptable behavior.

He's made comments that "women in America are different", and since he was preparing to immigrate to join his family in California, I was very explicit about how women in the West expect to be treated. He arrived a few months ago and seems to be doing well, and is actually pretty serious about joining the U.S. military, so I'm crossing my fingers that I helped him learn enough to break the cycle of misogyny that tends to permeate military society.

What is your favorite memory from your deployment experience?

All of that being said, I've had a great time on this deployment. I think the best part has been the feeling of camaraderie I've experienced. My last assignment was really hard on me, so being here, in an environment where I thrive and work with good people, has just been a wonderful experience overall.

There are two specific instances that stand out.

The first was when I worked a tough issue and managed to get an answer and the resulting product quickly. My boss (an Aussie O-6) responded to the email (which included a bunch of our senior leaders) with "Well done, Emily*. If anyone has any questions, she'll be able to help you." Just that little bit of praise, in a digitally-public setting, was enough to make me misty-eyed.

Similarly, when a general officer gave someone else credit for my work, my boss corrected him by saying "actually, sir, the Captain has been leading the charge on this." Getting kudos in a public environment is not something I'd experienced in a while.

Oh, and I also elevated an issue to an Afghan two-star that had been ignored for years, and the President of Afghanistan ended up giving an order to make it happen. THAT was cool.

How long are you going to be deployed?

I was gone just under a year.

Did you face any struggles while serving in the military?

I detail that a bit below, but I'm a naturally emotional person, and it can sometimes be hard not to let my emotions take over. Professionally, I struggle with confidence, especially when I realize I do a lot of "faking it until I make it" and it usually just happens to work out.

That being said, I legitimately hated myself for a while because I would look at these cool, collected officers and wonder why I couldn't be more like them. There are admiring traits in someone and hoping to adopt some of them, and then there's obsessing over what you're not. I stopped working on my good traits and figuring out how to incorporate them into my life, and instead started sinking into "why am I not good enough?" It's a vicious cycle and didn't help that my leadership was continuously highlighting my flaws while failing to give me any reasonable feedback.

There was a period where I wasn't the best officer, and I knew it, but I wasn't in a good place, and instead of being supportive, my leadership just wouldn't lay off. I would bring up concerns (example: I'm a Captain Flight Commander, but for some reason I report to the civilian flight chief before going to my boss? Why?) and would be told that, not only did I not have the right to ask why this weird thing was the way it is, but if I kept asking there would be consequences. I literally adopted the life motto of "Strap yourself to the mast and keep your head down. If they don't hear you, they don't see you, and they can't get mad."

In that time, the boss and his second tried to get me to go to mental health, but they had LITERALLY just given the officers a speech about how mental health was the best way to get a crappy Airman out of the services. So yeah, there was no way I was giving them more ammo. I now know this to be false, because I am currently seeing mental health, but at the time, I was terrified they would screw me over.

I was also given a Letter of Counseling (LOC) my last day in the squadron before going to Squadron Officer School and then moving to my next assignment (Permeant Change of Station (PCS)), for things that had occurred literally months before. I was told at the time that "everything you touch falls apart" and

I didn't deserve to be getting my dream job. My boss threatened my to take away my next assignment and said, "If he had his way, I wouldn't be going anywhere." It took a senior leader in our chain of command to finally get him to lay off and let me move on, and I thank my lucky stars every day for that person.

So, I drove off to SOS, freshly receiving a LOC, wondering if I'd have to return to that miserable place. I could write a book about the crap I experienced. To be fair, some of it was self-imposed: as I struggled with mental health, I didn't have the most resilient attitude.

However, my Flight Commander at Squadron Officer School (a class for Captains in the Air Force) was the absolute best person for me to have at that point in my life. He was gruff but fair, and he really cared about us. I told him everything I just told you (and then some) and he helped remind me that not everyone is the same, and the best way to combat naysayers was to be the best I could be. But he did it in a non-condescending way, so supportive, that I left there with a completely new outlook on life and the Air Force. People at my base even noticed I carried myself differently, had a better complexion, and just seemed better. I credit that man with keeping me in the Air Force, and I hope to repay him by being the absolute best I can be.

If you faced any difficulties did any of your struggles directly relate to the fact you are a female?

Absolutely. As an example, I was once speaking with the aforementioned boss about some soreness I was feeling from lifting weights, he told me that I "don't need to be doing that" and "should focus on cardio". He was a big dude (stocky, not muscular) and said "guys like me lift weights. People like you hit the treadmill" (I'm also a larger, but not fat, woman). I was so flabbergasted I didn't even realize how inappropriate it was until later. I also learned later that the two other female officers experienced similar situations but didn't say anything about it because it was so internalized it was just easier to ignore. We were afraid to "cause waves" (there it is again...) and didn't seek support when it was happening, because we thought it was isolated to us.

Wow, that isn't right, I think sometimes in the moment we don't realize how bad things people say are. Is there any other situation you can think of that makes it hard to be in the military as a female?

Well, as I mentioned, I'm a big woman. I lift. I'm strong. I sometimes have people make comments about how I don't have to help with the lifting, moving furniture, etc. I don't find it insulting; rather, it's a misguided attempt at chivalry. I remind people that their care is appreciated, but unnecessary. The phrase has become, "I'm a strong independent woman who can carry this box! But if you could open the door for me, that'd be swell!"

Also, it's hard being single in the military, and it's definitely hard being a single woman. I see a lot of female leaders who seem married to their work, and I wonder if that's how I'm going to be. I'm trying to come to terms that I can't have everything, while also not completely giving up on the things I want. I don't think the military is good at dealing with single people, especially single women. When I applied for this job, with the aforementioned boss saying to me, "but don't you want to get married? Have kids? Have you thought about how being deployed for two years will affect your chances?" I straight up asked him if he would have the same concerns with another Lieutenant (his favorite). "It's just different", he said.

After that, during my move, I had to take leave to drop my pets (two cats and a dog) in two states with friends who would watch them during my training and deployment. I got crap for taking that time, and was told that I was "abusing the leave policy". I asked who the boss thought should be taking care of this, as it was well known that my closest family lived ten hours away.

I remember his response well: complete silence for a few moments, and then "...fair enough".

How did being in the military affect you as a person? Did it change you? Did you learn anything about yourself?

I've had my worst times and also my best times in the military. I dealt with severe depression (during my time working for the aforementioned commander) but also some of the greatest job satisfaction I think I'm likely to experience.

I learned that once I start doubting myself, it's hard to pull myself out of it. I also learned that I have a hard time expression healthy emotion and tend to latch on to any big emotion - happy, sad, angry - that lets me feel a big swirl of emotion. It's internal usually, so tough to see, but it can hinder my work.

Now that I know it's there, it's manageable. I also know that work is my safe space, and if I'm miserable there, I'm going to be miserable everywhere. That being said, I'm also learning how to not be such a people pleaser, to stand up for myself, and to believe in myself more.

Were you able to get support with dealing with your depression?

As I mentioned, my previous boss and his second-in-command crony recommended I go to mental health literally the week after they boasted how easy it would be to kick a trouble-making Airmen out using his mental health record, so no, I never sought mental health there (which was ironic, considering my best friend at that base was a psychologist).

Once I moved to the next assignment, I saw a therapist through Military One Source, but she basically just agreed with everything I said and didn't really help ground me if that makes sense. I stopped seeing her when I realized what I really needed was just to get away from that toxic environment and be my own person. I focused on introspection. I exercised more. I stopped

76

putting everyone else on a pedestal and learned that I need to really search for negatives in people. It helps me not see everyone else as perfect; rather, everyone is flawed, and we can still like each other even knowing the flaws. This has been immensely helpful in going forward. I will say that I still have bad days and even bad weeks, but I feel they're much more manageable than they were before, and are far less destructive to my mental health. I'm now seeing a licensed therapist through DoD Stress Management, and while we're in the early stages – mostly just me talking and her getting a sense of who I am and what makes me tick – I find I look forward to the sessions. I'm learning that I can't control other people, but I can control myself. Such a simple thing, but so important.

What is your favorite memory from your military experience?

Working the Hurricane Sandy recovery in New Jersey and my deployment to Afghanistan.

The satisfaction to help others or be a part of something bigger than yourself?

Both. I definitely feel like I'm part of something bigger now, seeing where Afghanistan was even five years ago versus where it is now. I also really enjoy helping others, and here, I can help others WHILE being part of something bigger. I'm living the dream! The often-frustrating, but sometimes highly-rewarding dream!

What did you do to help with Hurricane Sandy recovery?

I was one of three people in charge of the Reception Control Center, coordinating the arrival and support of first responders and emergency personnel for my base. I worked two days straight, sleeping on a cot in an empty office when I could, and fielding calls while the storm was hitting. I helped find lodging and food for the military, federal, and private organizations that showed up to help.

In the end, I actually made up a short presentation that our wing commander briefed to Congress regarding Joint Base McGuire-Dix-Lakehurst's support, and I've seen it a few times since when people do analyses of the response. I actually had the opportunity to correct a briefer one time when he misinterpreted a situation, and when he tried to talk over me, I told him he was using my slide and I was available if he had any questions. Smartass Second Lieutenant, I was.

What would you tell women who are considering joining the military?

There is misogyny, both internalized and overt. Don't let it become the status quo. Fight it. Stick up for yourself, because there won't always be someone to do it for you. Always remember that your fellow airmen are your reason for being there, and anyone who gives you any other reason should be treated with wariness.

L *isa* served on active duty in the United States Air Force in the Security Force career field until she reached the rank of Staff Sergeant (E-5). She has since left the military behind and is currently a full-time student. While serving in the Air Force she deployed multiple times. She was hand-picked to go to Iraq "because [she] was the most dependable [and] strong female."*

Why did you decide to join the military?

I decided to join because I wanted the chance to serve our country and I always looked up to those who sacrificed so much that I wanted to be like them.

Have you deployed to?

Eskan Village, Saudi Arabia.

Al Udeid, Qatar.

Al Asad, Iraq

What deployment was the most memorable?

Al Asad, Iraq

What was the hardest part of being deployed?

Being one of the first twelve United States Air Force Security Forces members to be deployed at this location to provide security and law enforcement for other branches and countries was quite an unforgettable experience. We had to build our own buildings, furniture, etc., from scratch and from trash piles. We started a unit from absolutely nothing under wartime conditions. We also were not "technically deployed there" (we were a well-kept secret) Congress did not allot for us to be there and funding was also not allotted for us, meaning we did not have the vehicles, gear, tools, etc. that was necessary for our mission.

This base was originally a US base that was given back to Iraq then it was taken over by Islamic State in Iraq and Syria (ISIS) and we ended up coming back to fight against them in the Battle of Mosul. (Marines and Army were not trusted to provide law enforcement and security for the aircraft and personnel coming onto the base, so we were treated like outcasts).

It was difficult being one of only two females in my unit. We stuck together as much as we could, but we were on opposite shifts. There were no days off and the only thing we had to look forward to was food (when I say food, I mean stuff that looks like food but tastes just awful). Even then we ran out of food most days especially on Thanksgiving and Christmas and sometimes we had to resort to Meal Ready to Eat (MREs) or whatever we had left over.

Did you experience any differences between the culture of the US and the various countries you visited? What were they?

Yes, the culture was different in each location I visited.

In Saudi Arabia, the Saudi men were very flirtatious with the American women and would always bring us gifts from off-base and try to find us on Facebook. While the women I encountered were very rude they would purposely cut us off in lines, bump into us, and make it clear we were not welcome.

In Qatar, the culture was less strict it was more normal for the people to see Americans, but they still treated us differently. In Iraq, the Iraqi soldiers were very stern and distant with both the men and women in my group. They also didn't follow the rules of the base and caused many incidents. We were not sure how they felt about us, but we were always on guard while I was deployed in Iraq.

Was your job the same each time you deployed?

I was Security Forces law enforcement and security. My job was almost the same everywhere I was deployed.

What is your favorite memory from the deployment?

I can't think of one favorite memory, but I guess my favorite would be when my flight sergeants told me they were forward deploying me to Iraq because I was the most dependable/strong female (granted there were over 80 females to choose from). I didn't know whether to take this as a compliment or as an insult to my fellow airmen. :)

Did you face any challenges deployed because you were a female?

Always, my career field was predominately male and there were always jokes made to me about women in general. I grew thick skin and after a while, I just went with it to make them stop. After all, they really can't make fun of me after proving them wrong in many ways.

What struggles did you face while serving in the military?

The effects of wearing heavy gear have worn down my knees and back. It is not normal to carry that much weight on a daily basis. I also struggled with missing major events like my sisters' engagements and my nephews' births, etc.

Did any of your struggles directly relate to the fact you are a female?

Yes, I was misjudged and taken as a joke because of other females and their actions/attitudes.

What sort of things did other females do that made it, so you were not taken seriously?

Many other females would complain and say they could not do something because they were a woman. This obviously made me mad because they signed up for it and I was doing everything in my power to keep up with the other men.

Were you able to overcome any of these stereotypes?

Yes, my unit knew that I was different from my personality and actions.

What is the hardest part of being a female in the military?

Respect!

How did being in the military affect you as a person? Did it change you? Did you learn anything about yourself?

It changed me in many ways. After going through everything I have I look at it all as proof that I can and will overcome any obstacle and to take everything good and bad as a lesson. I also feel I am more grateful in general.

What changed you the most while being deployed?

Seeing how other cultures live and being deprived of so many freedoms really has made me more grateful for everything we have as Americans.

What is your favorite memory from your military experience?

Getting some serious air driving a High Mobility Multipurpose Wheeled Vehicle (HMMWV) in training...while I may have had fun the guy in the turret would say otherwise. :)

If you are married, did your spouse serve while you were in/is he serving now?

Not married, boyfriend served and deployed at same times as me but in different locations and with his reserve unit.

Did you face any challenges dating someone who was also in the military?

Yes, especially since my boyfriend was a rank higher than me, I received lots of judgment and comments about our relationship. When you join the military, the military thinks that they have the right to criticize your life decisions and choices. It is sad but it was almost easier to tell people I was not dating so they would not pry into my personal life.

Did you face any challenges since you were both deployed to different locations?

Yes, it was hard to stay in communication during my last deployment. I had little to no internet and letters and packages took months to arrive or deliver.

What would you tell women who are considering joining the military?

I would tell them that they will gain so many opportunities that the outside world can't offer and that their point of view on life will forever change especially after they have deployed.

*E*lizabeth* is currently serving as a Captain on active duty in the United States Air Force as a Pilot. She is married to a pilot who is also serving in the Air Force. Because they are not assigned to the same aircraft, they have been unable to be stationed together. Her story shows the real-life challenges military couples sometimes face.*

Why did you decide to join the military?

To fly fighters

Where have you deployed to?

Djibouti

How was the culture different from the United States in Djibouti?

We weren't in too much contact with the locals and weren't allowed off base. I did have a lady at the coffee shop ask me for my lunch box which I thought was odd. I ended up giving it to her, she gave me a free coffee in exchange. All the people I did come into contact with were very friendly and genuine.

Were you treated differently while deployed because you were a female?

Somewhat, not intentionally. The lodging refused to lodge me in the same area as my crew because the female bathroom wasn't as close as the other location. So, I ended up having to walk over a mile to do anything with them and get to work and that was pretty frustrating.

What is your favorite memory while deployed?

My husband also got deployed to the same location for a couple of weeks. It was the longest time we've been able to spend together. We didn't get to be housed in the same lodging, but it was just nice to have a routine with him and spend my days off with him. It was really a unique deployment experience!!

Did you face any struggles while serving in the military?

Yes- I'm not here doing what I wanted to do. I don't feel like I fit in personality wise. I constantly blame myself for not getting what I wanted. It also keeps me apart from my spouse because he is where I wanted to be.

What disqualified you from getting to do what you wanted to do?

I didn't do well enough in pilot training to obtain one of the very limited fighter spots.

Why do you blame yourself?

I could have done more to be better.

Why do you feel like your personality doesn't fit with your current career?

I don't really know. Just most of the people that I currently interact with I just don't relate to very well and vice versa. I get made fun of sometimes for marrying a fighter pilot and having wanted to be a fighter pilot. No one seems to be able to understand, and when they don't understand they just make jokes. Which I get, I do the same thing sometimes. I also sometimes feel like people walk on eggshells around me like I'm going to be offended if they say something. And I don't get any of that from my husband's coworkers.

If you faced any difficulties did any of your struggles directly relate to the fact you are a female?

Yes- I often get singled out. Most of the time not in a malicious way but I still hate it. I don't want to be treated like I'm different.

That is understandable. What sort of ways were you singled out? Do you think that it was done on purpose or just happened?

I think it's just the nature of things. Often when I go on TDY (military trips or training) they house me away from my crew. They don't make women's flight uniforms and my squadron doesn't have the flight uniforms that fit me in stock, we always have to order them. Other things include me getting scheduled to do things that is visibility with high ranking people. People ask me weird questions, like if I'm being "accommodated for appropriately" and "what's it like being a female pilot?" I've also been asked (not by a coworker) if I was going to just get pregnant so I could get out. I was appalled by that one. If/when I do get pregnant, I feel like it'll never be at a time when people will just be happy for me and not thinking I'm trying to get out of something. I just feel like I am way more under a microscope than other people. It motivates me to work really hard and put my best face on but it's exhausting and sometimes I just want to do my job and not be bothered.

How did being in the military affect you as a person? Did it change you? Did you learn anything about yourself?

I am definitely a more mature person for having been in the military. I think it really broadened my world view and made me strong. However, due to the many struggles that I've encountered, I would say I've become significantly bitter also, which is something I really don't like about myself.

What would you tell women who are considering joining the military?

I would definitely encourage them to. There are so many great career paths. But I would also tell them to not be picky about which one you want because while you can tell them what you want, and even if you're good enough to get it, the timing doesn't always work out and there aren't always options to try again later.

What is your favorite memory from your military experience?

Deploying to combat zones in Africa. I am rarely fulfilled with my job, but I enjoy the status that comes with going to combat.

If you are married, did your spouse serve while you were in/is he serving now?

My spouse and I both serve; we are both pilots I'm two different planes, so it makes getting us together really difficult. We still haven't lived together, and it will have been three assignments. We're both tired of being yanked around and treated like crap. And I'm tired if being treated like what I want for my career doesn't matter. That is probably the number one factor that will drive me out.

Being separated is really hard. I don't think people realize that being married in the military doesn't mean you will always be stationed together. What is the hardest part of being apart?

Just that people don't get it. I only get to see him for extended periods of time when we go on vacation together. The only side my coworkers see is me going on vacation frequently. They also somehow think that we make all this money both being in the military, but we don't live together so we have two houses, two cars, two sets of bills, etc. we're financially single. I just feel alone. I'm alone physically and I'm alone at work.

Would you have expected being separated as long as you have been when you joined?

I hadn't met him when I joined. When I joined, I was dating a civilian. It did not last very long after I joined.

How did you meet your husband?

In school

Do you think that people put his career ahead of yours because of the plane he flies or because you are a female?

No, there's a very large shortage in the fighter community and the Air Force is going to send them where they need him and he's not going to be able to leave the community even if he wanted to.

How much longer is your commitment to the military?

Another seven years

If you decided to get out would you be able to continue your career through joining the Reserves?

I do not know if I would, but I'd definitely look into it. I think it would depend on what unit would hire me and/or if my husband had also separated and/or if I would have to commute. I wouldn't do the reserves if I couldn't fly.

*K*ellie* is a Major serving on active duty in the United States Air Force. She is a Remotely Piloted Aircraft Pilot. Her husband is a civilian and follows her and her military career. He has found it hard to become a part of the military spouse culture and to find a job for his qualifications for each move they make.*

Why did you decide to join the military?

Help with college costs, ability to travel while serving, a career stepping stone

What was your career field/job?

Remotely Piloted Aircraft (RPA) pilot

What do you do as an RPA pilot?

I teach at the U.S. Air Force Weapons School.

Were you another career field before becoming an RPA pilot? If yes, what did you do?

I attended Euro-NATO Joint Jet Pilot Training then volunteered to RPAs as it was the only option that had a base where my husband could continue his career.

What struggles have you faced while serving in the military?

There's been a general lack of availability of medical care providers that were familiar with females and the inability for my husband to continue his career path at every duty station.

If you faced any difficulties did any of your struggles directly relate to the fact you are a female?

Yes (medical care required on base treatment, but on-base providers had little experience with treating female-specific issues and mainly tried medicating vs. finding a solution).

Were you able to get referred off base to get help with your medical issue?

With the exception of pelvic floor physical therapy, no. As an active-duty member on flight status, I am rarely referred off base.

What did you do to overcome this situation?

I have Endometriosis and it took my medical providers on base seven years to diagnose me. I had pain with sex, running, sitting, etc. and would bleed for weeks at a time, but when I would complain to my flight doctors, I was asked if I was being raped or having sex hanging from chandeliers. I was told to use lube, take it slow, and try new birth control.

For the first five years, I was put on a round of different birth control pills, all of which I absolutely hated using due to the hormonal side-effects. Each time I switched birth controls; I was not allowed to fly for a week. I eventually complained of pain and was bleeding for multiple months vs.five to eight days once a month that I was referred to Women's Health.

They also tried to give me birth control then offered medical menopause (hysterectomy) as a solution. When I said no, I was referred to a GI-tract doctor, who insisted I had something wrong with me and completed a colonoscopy and endoscopy. I felt the pain throughout both procedures and remember the doctor telling my husband as I was crying in pain in the recovery room that I should have children to fix my behavior.

I was then referred back to Women's Health when they didn't find anything wrong with my GI tract, and I was finally offered a laparoscopy which confirmed Endometriosis. After I was diagnosed with Endo, I was put on another round of birth control and only after requesting pelvic floor therapy after accomplishing my own research, was referred off base to a pelvic floor physical therapist. I have since stopped taking birth control, regained control of my hormones, and go to pelvic floor physical therapy to reduce pain.

Did you face any other struggles as a female in the military?

Yes. I have had to fight for women's rights at all my based locations, even when they are explicitly written into Air Force Instructions (AFIs). After my first child was born, there were no rooms in our all-male squadron for me to pump, so I pumped in the handicap bathroom (only bathroom with an outlet and room for a chair) for months until someone clogged up the toilet and it overflowed.

After complaining to the squadron commander, the only room available was his, so every time I needed to pump (three times a day, 20-min each) he was moved from his office. It was inconvenient for both of us. At my current location, it wasn't until I was on maternity leave that we had locations on base for nursing mothers to pump. Although prior to maternity leave I had asked my leadership which room I should use for pumping, it wasn't until I walked in with my child that my new commander informed me that I could use one of the briefing rooms and had a cypher lock installed on the door.

Initially, I was told to figure it out and find any open briefing room and put a sign on the door. The problem was, our briefing rooms are scheduled daily, so I would have to wait until the room was available verses a room being made available to me. I work in a male-dominated environment and the last civilian that attempted this was walked in on multiple times although she had a sign on the door and a chair pushed in front of it. Prior to going on maternity leave, I took the Air Force Instruction (AFI) regarding commanders making a safe, private room available to nursing/pumping mothers to the wing command chief, my commander, and four other commanders from various units in two separate wings. The command chief was very receptive and with his help as well as that of other agencies including the

99 ABW Chapel Team and the 57 WPSS, there are now multiple twenty-four-seven standing lactation rooms, including one in my current squadron.

Prior to leaving for maternity leave, my flight doc and I were able to change the medical waiver guide which restricted Remotely Piloted Aircraft (RPA) pilots from flying past 34-weeks of pregnancy without any medical rationale. Pregnant RPA pilots are now able to fly until 40-weeks' gestation, which is a huge win given the additional six weeks of flight time decreases the chances women returning from maternity leave will require a TDY (military training trip away from your family) to requalify in their aircraft.

How did being in the military affect you as a person? Did it change you? Did you learn anything about yourself?

Changed me for the better: learned a trade, leadership skills, mentorship opportunities both for others and myself, was able to complete a Masters in Science program, didn't pay out of pocket for either of my pregnancies or delivery, etc.

What is your favorite memory from your military experience?

Pilot training shenanigans

If you are married, did your spouse serve while you were in/is he serving now?

I am married, my spouse is a civilian.

Have your spouse faced any challenges being a male military spouse?

Yes, I'm the only female in my unit. While not necessarily a problem, it is a struggle for my husband and I for multiple reasons. Often, my husband has a difficult time finding a job every time we PCS as he's a Professional Engineer (PE) (electrical) with a Masters in Computer and Electrical Engineering from Georgia Tech.

Often, he's taken odd jobs just to stay busy. When we had asked the Airman and Family Readiness Center (AFR&C) and other base agencies for help, he's often overqualified for every job they are able to recommend and cannot be hired. We've tried all base resources and found them lacking in our situation as they're more geared toward people just starting careers and are typically not built for spouses with Top Secret / Sensitive Compartmented Information (SCIs), Professional Licenses, and Master's degrees.

It's also difficult for us to make friends as many female spouses are not welcoming to either my husband in the spouses' group or to me to hang out with them or their husbands. Spouses groups also have names that are not inclusive (Lady Bulls, etc.), address their emails to "Ladies," and when organizing events, gear them toward the stay-at-home spouse (9 am at Starbucks on a Tuesday). As a result, my husband rarely has any friends from within the military and is a highly qualified professional, so has difficulty finding work at smaller bases.

Is your spouse able to find a job easily as you move around with the military?

No. He's even been denied multiple jobs he's applied to because either they discriminate against military spouses and don't want to lose someone after two to three years, or he's overqualified for the work and they would not be able to compensate him appropriately.

What would you tell women who are considering joining the military?

It's a fantastic experience and career opportunity. I'd recommend using all services provided (Tuition Assistance, professional certificate, etc.) and to travel. It takes a toll on the family front, so expect to work through familial challenges (parents, significant other, children). Don't feel like you have to give the

Amanda Huffman

military more than the minimum years of service, they'll get their pound of flesh from you.

*M*ary* *is currently serving on active duty in the United States Air Force as a Staff Sergeant (E-5). She works as a maintainer and is working to get cross-trained into a new career field. Her husband is also serving in the military. Their life is about to change with a new arrival on the way.*

Why did you decide to join the military?

College benefits. I needed the education to pursue what I really wanted but didn't want the massive debt.

Where have you deployed to?

Once to Qatar, and once to Guam. Qatar was supposed to be for six months, I got sent home 1 month early because I needed extensive knee surgery. Guam was six months. I stayed the entire deployment.

What deployment was the most memorable?

Both were memorable for different reasons.

Guam was easier because it was less strenuous hours on the flight line. I also got to deploy with the man I am now married to. This deployment brought us even closer together and made us realize that we loved each other.

Qatar challenged me in every way possible. I had to learn how to overcome sexism, the rumors that were being made up about me, the horrible heat mixed with a heavy maintenance schedule and lazy coworkers. I learned a lot about myself and grew stronger. I also went through appendicitis and a really bad knee injury.

What was the hardest part of being deployed?

It's the feeling of being isolated and trapped. I can't just take leave and see family. You miss holidays and events. I hated constantly being surrounded by coworkers. While I was deployed to Qatar, I felt like I had no privacy and that I was constantly being bothered by horny men. When I turned down the men's advances, rumors started popping up that I was a "whore" and a "slut".

Did you experience any differences between the culture of the US and the various countries you visited? What were they?

The women in Qatar are primarily Muslim. I wasn't accustomed to covering everything up when it was hot out. Guam has a very welcoming environment. I went to the local market events. The food was phenomenal and the WWII history on the island was intriguing.

Was your job the same each time you deployed?

Aerospace Propulsion. Maintenance units deploy together with the airframe that they are assigned to.

What is your favorite memory from the deployment?

I went on a WWII tour of Guam on one of my days off with my now husband. We both enjoy history and enjoyed going to all the locations all over the island.

My favorite memory from my Qatar deployment was the long runs through the base. It was my time to think and be completely alone.

Did you face any challenges deployed because you were a female?

The only challenge I've really faced because I am a female is tampon-related. Thankfully, I packed enough to supply a small army. If I hadn't the BX's in Qatar and Guam didn't have the brand and size that I needed. I would have either had to gone without or have someone from the states send me some.

On both deployments, it was a long walk/drive depending on where the jets were on the line, to the bathrooms from the flight line. Qatar had some porta-johns, but they always had urine all over the toilet and no toilet paper when I entered them. I learned to bring disinfectant wipes and toilet paper with me.

What was your career field/job?

2A6X1F Aerospace Propulsion. It's the Air Force way of saying that I work on jet engines for the planes. I worked the B-1, GE F100 engines for four and half years and currently I work on F-16, PW 220 and 229 engines. It's like going from a Ford motor to a Toyota motor.

I recently applied for retraining as either: chaplain assistant, personalist or unit training manager. I should know whether it was approved or not within the next three to four months. It's a long waiting process.

Have you found out your new career field yet? What will your new career field be?

I did find out my new career field. It was supposed to be 3F2X1, unit training manager. (*There are no more open FTA quotas for chaplain assistant or personalist.*) I even had a tech school class start date for Unit Training Manager. The Air Force Personnel Center and the Career Field Manager rescinded their approval decision I can't give many details/specifics because I have gotten the Inspector General involved and I'm currently working through that process.

Hopefully, this can all be fixed, and my original class dates reinstated. It's a lot of unknowns and I feel wronged by the Air Force and the retraining process. It's really frustrating to have come this far and be treated like this.

What are you most excited about for this next job?

I was excited about this job because it is a different side of the Air Force. I didn't want to balance a new baby and a grueling career in maintenance any longer. I've stayed out of trouble and I've made the mission happen. I was excited for the opportunity to retrain and if it was accepted, I was excited to be reenlisting.

Did you face any struggles while serving in the military?

Earlier last year, I had orders to Korea before join spouse kicked in and kept my husband and I at the same base. I am at my second base and learning a new aircraft/engine has been frustrating. I'd say that my biggest struggle was learning that the rest of the Air Force does not function on maintenance timelines and that there are not a lot of good NCO's out there.

What do you mean by maintenance timelines?

Maintenance timelines are how much time it takes to fix a jet and get it crew ready. If your shift starts at 0700, you are expected to have tools checked out and ready and to get on that truck after roll call. 0700 in the maintainer world means that you and others in your shop show up at 0630-ish, gets turn over from the previous shift, prints off a 380 from cams, look at the flying schedule and gets ready for maintenance to begin.

Roll call is in Air Battle Uniforms and begins promptly at 0700, then you are expected to get on the truck and relieve the previous shift from the line. It can take anywhere from mere minutes to weeks to fix a jet. There are three shifts so there is twenty-four-hour coverage during the week. The work sometimes doesn't halt for the weekend. A weekend duty crew will come in and pick up where swing shift left off on Friday. Mistakes are taken very seriously because the pilot that flies that jet could lose his life if something wasn't repaired or inspected properly. Aircraft history learns from such awful events.

As a new Airman, I thought that all the other Airmen I saw in the Base Exchange, Medical Group, Finance, Military Personnel

Flight (MPF) all worked the same hours I did, just not in the outdoor elements like I did. I also thought that they were held to the same standards of performance that I was.

I got frustrated when finance messed up my paperwork when I returned from deployment and the only thing that his supervisor could tell me is that it was no big deal and to go see Airman Family Readiness. I didn't understand because mistakes at my work usually result in Letter of Reprimand or an Article 15. I didn't understand MPF wasn't ready to see customers 0730 or even 0750 when the sign on the door said they opened at 0730. I used to pray that the Medical Group had an early morning appointment when I was mid-shift so I wouldn't have to get my sick-self up in the middle of my sleep schedule or go to the Emergency Room before mid-shift started. No other non-maintenance office/shop on base (except for security forces and occasionally Civil Engineers) worked hours outside of 0700-1630. It was frustrating to get appointments taken care of because my work hours different from all the places my appointments were.

How is the rest of the Air Force different than the maintenance career field?

It's eight to sixteen hours either in the extreme heat or extreme cold doing physical work on an aging jet. Training and training records are taken very seriously. Mistakes could result in damage to aircraft, serious injury or death to personnel. One of the good things that come from an environment like this is comradery. It's hard not to bond with maintainer next to you when you are trying to fix a jet and your hands are literally frozen to the tools. I can basically describe the comradery like a dysfunctional family, but a family, nonetheless. Every family has a couple of cruel jerks in the bunch. I've encountered a lot of sexist men, but for every two to three sexists, there's a good one that gives me the respect and the credit I deserve as an Airman and a maintainer.

If you faced any difficulties did any of your struggles directly relate to the fact you are a female?

I faced sexism from two men on my first deployment. I was going through a lot that the first deployment. I was recently divorced, lonely, stressed, and overworked. It didn't help when I got appendicitis and two months later, I had to be sent home after a severe knee injury I got when I slipped on oil while at work. I also faced it when I first came into the flight line.

How does a deployment cause normal stress to intensify?

There's isn't enough time to decompress and relax before your next shift. Stress from the previous day rolls right into the new day. It's a vicious cycle.

How were you able to adapt and overcome to survive your deployment experience?

I wouldn't call it survival. I call it being resilient and pushing through. I remember being at basic training and our Military Training Instructor telling us that basic is just temporary. I took that to heart, and it's become my motto for the past five years that I have been in. I won't be deployed forever. Eventually, I get to come home. I changed my focus to just one day at a time and before I knew it, it was time to go home and I welcomed the relief that I felt from that.

Do you think the climate is changing in regard to sexual harassment or do you think women will continue to face challenges in the military?

I think that the climate regarding sexual harassment is changing for the better. Zero tolerance is making its way through the ranks. I don't think it will ever be eliminated because there is no way to screen for all predators before they enlist. However, the military is taking all complaints seriously and it is handled.

I think women will always face sexism, especially in a career field like maintenance. I do think that some females make it harder on other female maintainers when they don't pull their weight on the line. It's better than it was when I first came in, but I don't know if it's because I have become thick-skinned and proficient at my job or if it's because the culture is changing.

How did being in the military affect you as a person? Did it change you? Did you learn anything about yourself?

Honestly, maintenance changed me. I grew thick skin and for the first time in my life, I learned how to stand my ground and pull my weight. I learned that I am a very tactile and visual learner. I also learned how to learn quickly. The military has taught me that no matter how tired I am, I still have more to give. The most important thing that I have learned is that I am someone that will always care.

What would you tell women who are considering joining the military?

Do NOT go into maintenance. Save yourself from the tears, the safety wire injuries and the twelve to sixteen-hour days, plus weekend duty. Be prepared to work harder than the men beside her in order to earn the respect she deserves, don't sleep with her coworkers and be prepared for everyone to tell her that every award she's earned is because she's a female.

What do you think a better career field would be? And why?

Any job that is primarily an admin/desk job and predominantly female. I don't want anyone to have to go through the things that I've had to go through in the maintenance career field.

What is your favorite memory from your military experience?

Serving in the base honor guard as an A1C. I discovered that I really enjoyed this way to say thank you and honor those that served before me. A lot of the memories that I am fond of are the ones that redirected my thinking and encouraged me to keep pushing through.

If you are married, did your spouse serve while you were in/is he serving now?

He is still serving. He is a Staff Sergeant as well and he is a unit training manager now (3F2X1, formally 3S2X1). He retrained out of maintenance about a year ago. He spent five years a B-1 crew chief (2A5X1, I forget his shred out letter).

Did you face challenges as you both served in the military?

Our main challenge is our work schedules. His hours are the same Monday-Friday. He works day shift hours. He doesn't ever have to work on weekends. My work hours change based on the flying schedule and that changes every week. I also have a weekend duty from time to time. I am not always on day shift. I was on mid-shift for a year and a half at my last base and for most of my time at this base until I got pregnant. My shop switches up who's on what shift based on who is on leave, in a class, etc. and where we need our experienced workers, so we can fix the jets effectively. For most of our relationship, we've been on opposite shifts. I am currently on day shift and off the flight line but it's only because I am pregnant. I have truly enjoyed getting to spend more time with him.

What was the hardest part of both you and your spouse being in the military?

Accepting the unknown and trying to plan our future. There is no guarantee that if we both stay in, that we will get orders the same base. I can't go to all the bases that he can because my job is for specific engines. Neither of us wants to have to decide "who gets the child" if we are stationed apart.

How did you and your spouse meet?

We met at our last base through the Honor Guard. We didn't date each other until a couple of years after that. I ran into him outside of work on my birthday and ended up talking. Before we knew it, we were dating and living together. We clicked and it feels like fate.

How do you think your life will change when your new arrival comes?

I think everything will change but I think that it's a good thing. We have no choice but to send our child to daycare and I know it will be my husband that will take the baby there most days. We will be tired a lot and frustrated. I think we will figure it out and will bring us closer together.

Do you think it will be harder to be in the military when you have children?

I think it will be harder. Even if I wasn't in maintenance, I wouldn't be able to raise my child the way that we really want to. If my retraining doesn't work out, we have already decided that me walking away from maintenance is the best option.

Amanda Huffman

*J*o Ann retired from the United States Air Force after 20 years of service in 1999. She served on active duty and retired as a Tech Sergeant (E-6). She began her career as a jet mechanic but was retrained to become a Personalist. She currently works as a Human Resource Admin Assistant at AIMS Community College.

Why did you decide to join the military?

My parents had decided to move to Alaska right after I graduated high school, my job at the time didn't pay enough for me to move out. My dad suggested I go into the military. I didn't want to but felt like I had no choice.

Wow, was it hard for you to feel like you were forced into the military?

It was very difficult. I felt a little abandoned. I didn't communicate with my parents for the first two months I was in. They didn't end up going to Alaska, however, they did sell our house, and my car, and moved to another city.

Why did you decide to choose the Air Force?

My dad retired from the Air Force and my oldest sister was in the Air Force when I enlisted.

Have you deployed?

To Hurlburt field FL for Bold Eagle 85

What is Bold Eagle 85? What did you do? How long?

It was a joint military exercise based out of a field at Hurlburt Field, it included Air Force, Army and I believe there were some Marines. We erected a tent city where we lived for about three weeks. Shower tent, chow tent, sleeping tents. My job, as military personnel was to account for every troop that came in and out of tent city. We were responsible for reporting "casualties" and "injured". We maintained communication with each troops home base.

What was your career field/job?

When I went to pick a job, they were only offering mechanic or fuel specialists to qualified women. I picked the lesser of two evils, jet engine mechanic. I did that for two years before I was medically retrained into military personnel.

Are you glad you made the switch to Personnel?

Absolutely! I did my best as a mechanic, but it just didn't come naturally to me.

What did you do as a jet engine mechanic?

I worked in the engine shop on KC-135 engines.

Did you face any struggles while serving in the military?

Definitely! My roommate and I were the first two to move into the male dorm. Very interesting!

Why did the Air Force choose to put males in female in the same dorm?

As more women began being assigned to the base, they had no choice because they did not have a dorm dedicated to women only. My roommate and I were given (as Airmen) a Jr Non-Commissioned-Officer room, which was larger than the regular rooms and we had our own bathroom.

Shortly after, we were reassigned to a smaller room that shared a bathroom with two guys. They smoked pot frequently and we would have to shove towels under the door to keep the smoke out of our room. The bathroom locked from the inside, so there was never any problem with being walked in on. The main issue was that they were slobs!

The one real issue we had was that the dorm manager was a male. When he would do room inspections (while we were at work), he would go through our stuff. I came home one day to find my nightgown draped over the lamp!

If you faced any difficulties did any of your struggles directly relate to the fact you are a female?

Absolutely! The day I reported to my first base I was told they didn't want women in the shop and if I wanted out, they would help me.

This must have made it hard to be in the Air Force. Were you able to get accepted into the machine shop or is this why you decided on a new career field?

I worked as hard as I could to be accepted, however, I also had medical issues. I suffered multiple stress fractures during basic training, and they weren't diagnosed until after I reached my first base (almost seven months later). I went through numerous types of therapy, including having each leg casted, one at a time.

This limited my capabilities and I was briefly assigned as the Technical Order maintenance person. Ironically, this required more walking and standing then my job did. I reported to a supervisor who had pictures of naked Korean women all over his desk. He made me walk, with a cast on my leg, to all the various shops to update their technical order books, then he would complain that I took too long.

How did being in the military affect you as a person? Did it change you? Did you learn anything about yourself?

As a very shy young eighteen-year-old, I was subjected to using a coed latrine! How embarrassing!!! I had to prove myself every day. I learned that I was much more determined than I realized because I dug in and did my best.

That is crazy. I had to use a coed bathroom while deployed,

but that was long into my service and it was inconvenient, but also a very different situation. How were you able to cope with some of these hard situations as a young eighteen-year-old?

I will never forget the first time I needed to go to the bathroom and asked where it was. I was directed towards the latrine, and I strolled in and, fortunately, went to one of the first couple of stalls. I heard someone come in, and as I exited the stall to walk over to the sinks, I couldn't help but notice that there was a man standing at a urinal, probably four feet from the sink area. I was so embarrassed and shocked!

One of the other women (there were only three of us) told me to make sure I always used only the first two stalls to avoid the direct view of the guys. I did my best to only use the restroom during my lunch break and before and after work.

Living in the coed dorm was quite an adventure. I was unaccustomed to such intense attention from guys. I, unfortunately, learned very quickly that the attention didn't mean they actually cared about you, but rather the fact that you were a female.

What would you tell women who are considering joining the military?

Today's military is so different from when I joined, I think they just need to be prepared for anything. Be bold, be confident and report ANY action that is inappropriate immediately.

I would agree. When were you in the Air Force?

I enlisted on 29 January 1979 and retired 1 February 1999.

What is your favorite memory from your military experience?

Winning awards at NCO Leadership School despite my lack of confidence.

If you are married, did your spouse serve while you were in/is he serving now?

I am recently widowed, but I did meet my husband in the service. He retired and followed me for almost ten years.

How did you meet your late husband?

He was my supervisor, right before he retired. He was a single dad, widowed four years prior to our meeting. We started dating and shortly after he retired, we got engaged. We were married for 28 years, and he followed me as a civilian for almost ten years.

While you were in was he able to support and understand some of the things you were going through since he had also served?

Yes, it was extremely helpful being married to someone who was prior military, he knew about military exercises, long hours, frustration, etc. I know quite a few women that married civilians and had difficulties because they couldn't relate to the stress of a military person.

J *ustine is currently serving on active duty in the Air Force as a Captain. She is a labor and delivery nurse.*

Why did you decide to join the military?

My family has a strong military background. I also did the Reserve Officer Training Corps (ROTC) and joined with a scholarship.

Where have you deployed to?

I did a two-week deployment to the Dominican Republic

What did you do in the Dominican Republic?

We performed medical/dental evaluations/treatment for the local population. We also gave them glasses/medications as needed (based on what we brought). We were only there for a couple of weeks; each day hundreds of people would line up to be seen.

What was your team's mission?

It was considered a "deployment training exercise," essentially making sure that if we needed to deploy, we would be able to. It was also aimed to help improve our Nation's relationship with the Dominican Republic.

Was the culture difference in the Dominican Republic compared to the US? How?

Many people were much more appreciative; they do not have access to healthcare that people in the US tend to take for granted.

Did you face any challenges while deployed?

Limited resources. We only had the equipment/supplies we brought with us. Also, some language barriers. I speak a minimal amount of Spanish; we had some translators, but we didn't always have as many as we needed.

What was your career field/job?

I'm a labor and delivery nurse

What is the coolest thing about working Labor and Delivery?

I am pretty passionate about my job. I think being a Labor and Delivery nurse is one of the best jobs to have. It is pretty incredible to watch women labor for hours on end to bring new life into the world. The delivery is my favorite part; seeing the new parents' faces of pure joy, love, bewilderment; it's a pretty incredible experience.

And how cool is it that these people invite you to be part of such an intimate moment in their lives? When they are in their most vulnerable state, and you get to be the one to provide the support they need, you can make or break this experience for them.

Did you face any struggles while serving in the military?

My husband is also military. The biggest struggle I've encountered is trying to spend time with my husband. We are both shift-workers, and our schedules often don't line up. Sometimes we'll go days without talking face-to-face because one of us will be sleeping when the other gets home and will leave before the other wakes up.

The other struggle is trying to get various training opportunities. I've been trying to go to a leadership course for about a year now, and have had difficulty (mostly due to staffing and rank)

How do you make the most of the time when you are together?

New development to this story: my husband is now deployed.

He left in April and will return late October.

To make the most of the time we have together, we just try to be near each other. Often times my husband has to bring work home with him, but he will take his laptop out of his office and bring it into the living room to sit with me.

Is there a way you guys stay connected when you don't get to see each other for a few days/weeks?

We will message each other, mostly over social media or texting. We always make sure to say goodbye to one another when we leave for work—even if the other person won't remember because they were half asleep when we woke them up for a kiss goodbye.

How did being in the military affect you as a person? Did it change you? Did you learn anything about yourself?

It has definitely made me a better person. It has taught me about sacrifice and putting the needs of the Air Force and the country before myself and what I want. It has taught me about the importance of being part of something bigger than myself. It has reinforced my love and appreciation of my family—I am currently living overseas and miss my family terribly. I could probably go on for hours about everything being in the Military has taught me.

What would you tell women who are considering joining the military?

Do it. Dive in, head first. You will meet some of the most incredible people, you will be given opportunities you never thought existed, and you will learn more about leadership than you could ever hope to learn. It will do nothing but help you grow in all aspects of your life. So, do it.

What is your favorite memory from your military experience?

Living in Germany has been amazing; I don't think I could pin-

Amanda Huffman

point one specific experience.

Have you had the opportunity to travel in Europe or Germany?

Yes! One of the coolest parts about being stationed here in Germany. I've been to twelve new countries and I've been here for just over a year. I have also been to quite a few places in Germany.

What is your favorite place you have visited?

My favorite place (so far) is Switzerland. I have never been emotionally moved by scenery until our drive to Switzerland. The Alps are quite literally breathtaking.

How did you and your husband meet?

We met at Field Training in the summer of 2012. ROTC is typically a four-year training experience, and (usually) during your sophomore year you attend Field Training. This is essentially the officer's version of "boot camp." The following year, I went back as a Cadet Training Assistant to help train the Cadets at Field Training. My husband also attended as a Cadet Training Assistant, and we ended up being in Sister Flights (which essentially means we worked together every day). We spent nine weeks for about 19-20 hours a day together and decided we liked each other.

Do you think you and your husband will both stay in for 20 years?

It is currently my goal to stay in the full 20 years. My husband has talked about possibly getting out when we have children to be a stay-at-home dad. But nothing has been decided yet! Too many unknown factors!

What advice would you give to couples who are dual military?

We have only been married for two years, so I don't have a ton of advice! So far, we both really enjoy our jobs and are lucky to be stationed together. However, we did a lot of long distance while we dated, and I am sick of that. So, if the military ever told us we had to be stationed away from each other, one of us would probably get out.

You need to decide what is important for you and what your top priorities are. My husband is my number one priority. At the end of the day, I come home to my husband, not my job. I can always get a new job but wouldn't dream of getting a new husband.

L indsay is a mom, wife, veteran, logistician, and owner of *MilSO Box LLC. Since separating from the Air Force, she has continued her logistics experience through civilian positions while seeking meaningful entrepreneurial opportunities. When a childhood friend, now an Army wife and mom, expressed her troubles during a phone call, Lindsay decided to create a business that could bring joy to her and the thousands of women like her. In 2016, she founded MilSO Box LLC, a subscription box company that curates gift boxes for the female military significant others (MilSO's) of our troops. To further support the military community, she is dedicated to sourcing each box's products from Veteran-owned, MilSO owned, and/ or military family owned businesses. In 2018, Lindsay expanded this secondary mission by establishing gifting-withvalor.com.*

Why did you decide to join the military?

I needed to find a way to pay for college and was awarded an Air Force ROTC scholarship. I also thought that serving in the military would be exciting, a chance to see the world and be badass defending our country. Both of my parents were in the Air Force and encouraged me to join as well.

Have you deployed?

No, I never deployed. My active duty career was short-lived, and I was stationed at Hickam AFB, HI where we were considered "forward deployed." Our mission was to move personnel and cargo through the Pacific.

What was your career field/job?

I was placed in logistics and began as a Deputy Flight Commander of Cargo Operations. I also did rotations in the Air

Traffic Operations Center and in Passenger Operations. By the time I separated, I was the Executive Assistant to the Squadron Commander.

Did you face any struggles while serving in the military?

The struggles I faced were mostly with my identity and my impatience.

Up until college, I was known as a performer in music and theater. I practically lived on stage. Even in college, ROTC did not fully take over my identity. However, when I began active duty, no one knew my past, my personality, or what really made me ME. Being an Officer meant that I had to be very professional and a leader, which I was. However, it was a challenge to present myself in a way I felt was one-dimensional. I am naturally very silly, crazy (in a fun way,) and very open-minded. Being an Air Force Officer made me feel stifled. I had no creative outlet and felt trapped.

My impatience reared its ugly head as soon as I arrived at my duty station. I was ready for action. I at least wanted to be useful and help in any way I could. Instead, I had nothing to do, and knew nothing about the job I was placed in. The two months I waited to go to tech school felt like such a waste of time that I created my own training program and published it for any future officers who came into my position. I'm sure that a lot of junior officers feel useless and uninformed when they first join, but my impatience made it insufferable.

If you faced any difficulties did any of your struggles directly relate to the fact you are a female?

I don't believe the fact that I was female directly related to any struggle except my loneliness. I was married to a civilian and didn't feel comfortable becoming too close with any of the male junior officers. The few female junior officers in my squadron were moms, and I felt we had very little in common. Since

I was unable to fraternize with any enlisted personnel, it was very lonely.

How did being in the military affect you as a person? Did it change you? Did you learn anything about yourself?

I learned a lot about myself through my experience. Mostly, I learned that I was more dedicated to my family than to serving my country. I'm sure that makes me less of a hero, but my experience solidified my priority to put them first. My mom was dying while I was gone. Her kidneys had stopped functioning, and only a kidney transplant could save her. I was able to fly home for the transplant, but I could not be there for her while she was at her worst. She has made a full recovery, but I could never again put myself in a position that prevented me from being there for the people who matter most in my life.

On a positive note, I found that I am an excellent marksman. I also learned that the only way to effectively gain the respect of others is to give respect first. The senior Non-Commissioned Officers in the military are absolutely its backbone. If an officer is not willing to recognize their value or listen to their advice, they frankly do not deserve their commission. Attention to detail is so important in the military, and I still use that skill every day. Lastly, the people who are willing to risk their lives for our country are true heroes who should never be forgotten.

What would you tell women who are considering joining the military?

The fact that you are female should not be a limiting factor except in a few career specialties. Of course, there are naysayers, but they can provide great motivation for you to be an even bigger badass and prove them wrong. Never use your gender as an excuse. Use it as a strength that your male counterparts lack. No person can possibly do or know everything, but women are more likely to admit it, learn, and grow.

What is your favorite memory from your military experience?

My favorite memory from the military is my tech school experience. Our class was 40 strong, and we were thick as thieves. I made a few friends there that I will have for life, and we connected as young officers who knew nothing, but wanted to be the best we could be.

If you are married, did your spouse serve while you were in/is he serving now?

My husband and I were married one week before I commissioned as an Air Force Officer. He has never served.

ARMY

L *ynda retired from the United States Army after 20 years on active duty as a Sergeant. She deployed multiple times during her military career.*

Why did you decide to join the military?

There has always been someone every generation in the military in my family.

Where have you deployed to?

Saudi Arabia - twice

Iraq - twice

Kuwait - once

Wow, five deployments. I'd love to hear a little more about them.

I was in Desert Storm for my first time in Saudi. The second time I was an augmentee to take over the switch job from the Air Force to the Army.

The first time in Iraq, I was the communications support for a Personal Security Detail (PSD) team as well as driving a bus to and from Victory Base Complex (VBC) and Baghdad International Airport (BIAP). The second time in Iraq, I was a supply Sergeant for a security team and then on the second half of my tour, I was working with Morale Welfare and Recreation (MWR) in handling the entertainers that came in country.

The time I went to Kuwait was in support of Operation Enduring Freedom and I was a team chief for a Communications Relay Group (CRG) for an Air Defense Artillery (ADA) unit.

What was you or your team's mission?

The first time in Saudi Arabia I was supposed to go over to be a communications specialist. I ended up being a truck driver. I convoyed supplies up and down the area. The second time, my team was involved in getting a switch from Dubai to Dhahran and convert it from the Air Force responsibility to Army. This included installing a Red IST line in the switch (it was basically the "bat line" to the Pentagon). First time in Iraq, I was originally just a bus driver but when there was a PSD team that didn't have any communications support, I volunteered to be theirs. I was in charge of programing the Roles of the Blue Force Tracking and making sure they were up to date.

The second time in Iraq, I was to ensure that the security detail had everything that they needed to complete their mission. We were there to change over from Operation Iraqi Freedom (OIF) to Operation New Dawn (OND). When that was completed, I went to work for the MWR in greeting the entertainment (like Five Finger Death Punch, Vertical Horizon, Nathan Lee Band, etc.) and to make sure that they were comfortable and got to the correct places at the times they were to be.

In Kuwait, I was a team chief of a CRG, which works with an ADA system.

What was your job?

Each day to day task was different. The easiest way to put it, was to ensure that the mission was completed and successful.

What cultural differences do you remember between the country you went to and the United States?

I remember the second time in Saudi Arabia, I had to wear an abaya if I went off-site. If there was a male in the vehicle, I couldn't drive, and I had to sit in the back seat. Also, if we were going out to eat, I had to make sure that it was a family establishment otherwise I couldn't go in. I had to use a male soldier to tell the contractors what to do because I was a female. I also had to be aware of the "religious police" when off-site.

Did you face any challenges while you were deployed?

The main challenge that I faced while deployed was going out on missions and if going to an all-male Combat Outpost, I had to make sure that I had a "battle buddy" with me. I was the only female in my unit at the time to be going out as far as we did. The was to include going to "The Devil's Triangle" and Muhammadi-yah and other outlying areas. That and making sure you had shampoo and conditioner. Most times the Army and Air Force Exchange Services (AAFES) shop only had shampoo.

Did you face any challenges while you were deployed because you were a female? If yes, what were they?

The biggest challenge that I had was getting the respect from the other guys I worked with on each tour. It helped with my first tour to Iraq that beforehand I was stationed with light in-fantry in Hawaii, so I knew how those guys worked. It also helped that I was always the only female on my teams. I was in a male dominant Military Occupation Specialty (MOS) code.

What is your favorite memory from your deployment experi-ence(s)?

My favorite memory was one that I didn't have a part in. It was seeing the destruction that the Iraq war had caused to cities but while driving through one city, I remember seeing the children clearing a trashed field so that they could play soccer in. To be able to see that the children could still take time to be children and just play was awesome.

What sort of struggles did you face?

Then there were the times that the guys couldn't believe that I could shoot a perfect 40 out of 40 at the range. Then there were the times when some leaders would dismiss me because they didn't think that I could have the correct answer for the problem.

How did you overcome these struggles?

I worked hard, I was always truthful, and I fought for my Soldiers and I never asked them to do anything that I wasn't willing to do. If they were putting up camouflage, I was out there putting it up also. I never backed down. I proved my worth.

How did being in the military affect you as a person? Did it change you? Did you learn anything about yourself?

Being in the military made me into an independent, strong woman.

What would you tell women who are considering joining the military?

To believe in yourself.

What is your favorite memory from your military experience?

Being able to get a switch working that no one else could get working.

Why is that your favorite memory? Is there more to the story?

When stationed in Hawaii, I was originally on a Forced Entry Switch (FES). In fact, I had to teach myself how to work it and then teach my soldiers. But I had a Platoon Sergeant (who used to be my Section Sergeant and I made him look bad in one instance) and he decided to put me on a Dismounted Extension Switch (DES). The DES basically is a portable switch that can be on the back of a truck or in a cave, if need be. But in my unit, none of them worked. So, I spent many hours after and during work to get the switch online. I finally did it and it impressed the higher-ups (not my Platoon Sergeant). I found out after I made a Permanent Change of Station to Korea, that the Company Sergeant Major of the Battalion wanted me back because they stripped the DES's and could not get them to work again.

They wanted me back because they knew that I could get them working again.

The reason that the Platoon Sergeant didn't like me was because on 9/11, we were pulled in from the field and were waiting to see what would happen with us. We were the only tactical signal unit in the Pacific. While waiting I asked my then Section Sergeant if I could go to my room and drop off my training Mission Oriented Protective Posture (MOPP) gear. He goes, "Oh no, we might need that." I told him that the training suit would not even stop gas. He then drags me to the Platoon Sergeant and tells him what I requested.

The Platoon Sergeant looks down at my right sleeve (at my combat patch) and then looks at the Section Sergeant and told him, "Since she already has a combat patch, I would think that she knows what she is talking about. I would listen to her." Needless to say, that didn't go over well and was never forgiven for making him look like a fool. Before this, he was a recruiter for a number of years.

If you are married, did your spouse serve while you were in/is he serving now?

Divorced.

Was your x-husband in the military?

My ex was in the military. He is also retired.

Did the military cause challenges make it hard to stay together?

It made it difficult to spend any time together since I was in more of a tactical job than him. Also, me getting Post Traumatic Stress Disorder didn't help at all either. It made things very difficult for him. But we are still friends.

*R*olande Summer served in the United States Army on Active Guard Reserves in Human Resources and as a Heavy Vehicle Officer until she was medically retired.

Why did you decide to join the military?

I joined the military because I wanted to pay for college. My mom was a single parent and couldn't afford to send both my sister and I to college. Since I was in Jr ROTC in high school, the military seemed like a natural choice for college tuition. I chose the Army because I was too weak to lift the bar in the Air Force physical, I couldn't swim so the Navy was out. The Marines was never an option, I wasn't tough enough, LOL. The Army said they would make me a Soldier from where I was, weak and all.

Have you deployed? If yes, where?

Yes, Afghanistan.

What was your job in Afghanistan?

I was the equivalent of a Human Resource Manager and I was an Acting Platoon Leader

What cultural difference did you notice between Afghanistan and the US?

There was so little, but the people seemed content. The homes were made of rock and everyone walked. It was odd to see someone in a car or in modern clothing. I learned just how spoiled and arrogant I was while I served over there.

Did you face any challenges overseas?

Yes, but nothing unusually different than anyone else. We actually stayed in a good location. Most of us had our own rooms in these little wooden buildings. The water was full of chlorine and we stayed about ½ mile away from a poop pond. However, it could have been worse.

Do you have a memory from your deployment experience?

I have lots of memories. They usually come to me in flashbacks. My most pleasant memory is of wing night. Wing night was like a taste of home. I really enjoyed my time in the gym. Working out really seemed to relieve the stress.

What was your career field/job?

Human Resources and Heavy Vehicle Operator

What did you do in Human Resources?

I took care of the Soldier's personal matters. Processed paperwork for career advancement, evaluations, urinalysis testing, and other administrative matters.

What does ah Heavy Vehicle Operator do?

I drove a type of cargo truck and generally as a fill-in operator. I only went on three or four trips. Most of them were fun and an opportunity to see the country. I drove with some of the best operators around. I felt safe.

Did you face any struggles while serving in the military?

Yes, it seemed like male leaders chose not to take me seriously until I proved how valuable I was to the team. Even still, many were threatened by my no-nonsense way of doing business.

Was this something that continually happened when you had new leadership come in?

It felt like it. I'm sure I didn't help by not acting girly and sweet.

If you faced any difficulties did any of your struggles directly relate to the fact you are a female?

Absolutely! Being an African American woman at that seemed to intimidate quite a few men.

What ways were you able to overcome these struggles?

I kept pushing forward and helping as many people as I possibly could. That made me feel good about my service. I tried to take in as much of my surroundings when I traveled. I felt pretty blessed to have a job that compensated me so well. It afforded me and my family the life we have today.

How did being in the military affect you as a person? Did it change you? Did you learn anything about yourself?

I am a stronger and less sheltered person. I'm more open-minded and willing to try new things. I developed a strong work ethic.

What would you tell women who are considering joining the military?

Don't be afraid to stand up for what is right. Don't be afraid to say no. Love who you are no matter what anyone says to you.

What is your favorite memory from your military experience?

My favorite memories consist of traveling with friends to different locations. It was fun to experience something new with people you shared a bond with.

If you are married, did your spouse serve while you were in/is he serving now?

No, my husband didn't serve. He was one of the rare service husbands. He was and is a strong man to be supportive of my dream of defending my country. Most men who didn't serve have a hard time with a woman happily working in such a masculine career.

*L*aura Jackson served in the Army Reserves for three years from 1975 to 1978. She was an Army medic and her job was to take care of veterans and their family members. She left the Army at the rank of Specialist (E4).

Why did you decided to join the military?

To serve/become a nurse/medic and help others

Do you think joining the Army allows you to do this?

Totally. It gave me my living security, direction, a career and a purpose, as well as a paycheck!

What was your career field/job?

Army medic/Nurse working at various places such as: Brooke Army Medical Center, Aberdeen Proving Grounds, VA Providence, RI.

What do you do as an Army Medic?

I cared mostly for veterans and their family members. I also was a case manager for some and served them taking vitals, distributing medications, giving shots, IV's, catheters, care and comfort, etc.

What sort of struggles did you face while serving in the military?

I was attacked in a barrack and out on drills by other black female soldiers who ganged up on me while attending my first AIT 91B10 at Ft. Sam Houston, San Antonio, TX. They would position themselves in back of me in line ups and kick my shins as we marched anywhere, we were going.

Then a group of them ganged up on me in the barracks near

the phone booth where we were allowed to make a phone call. Three soldiers knocked me down on the floor, kicked me in my stomach and hit me in the head.

At this time, we were living in the very large open bay barracks with community showers, etc. with huge rooms lined with bunk beds on both sides of the room.

This is how I met Zinha. She happened to come by and saw what was happening. She screamed at the girls attacking me and yanked them off me. From then on Zinha protected me and I was allowed to move my bunk to be close to hers. She was like a body guard for me after that.

We were both assigned to go to 91C20 training for nursing school. Zinha and I moved together and we were living in a very small, old barrack building with rooms that had one shared bathroom between us. Shortly after we moved in the barrack, it was scheduled to be fumigated due to it being infested with cockroaches. The largest cockroaches were about 3 inches long as I recall. The cockroach families (as I called them) would crawl everywhere...even under my pillow, bedding, across my desk, throughout the community kitchen, in the refrigerator, on the walls, floors, etc. They would run and scatter quickly when we turned on a light. I had never seen a cockroach in my life before this.

After the weekend barrack fumigation, we returned to live in the barrack. A few weeks later, my friend, Zinha, (now I call her my Army mom and my angel) began to complain of headaches and even migraines and I began to struggle to get any sleep. I had severe insomnia and after three days and nights of NO sleep, I was losing my ability to think clearly and became anxious. It was also the year of the Cicadas, so locust began to scream and scream a high pitch in unison starting at three or four in the morning till well after daybreak.

At my 91C20 AIT, Captain Kris asked our Master Sergeant to take me to the mental health clinic. There he dropped me off at the door. I met with a Staff Sergeant. He began to question and question me despite my many attempts to share that I just needed to sleep and that I could not think anymore. I shared that I was top tenth honor graduate student in my high school and that I had been a dancer, gymnast, etc. He gave me a prescription for Thorazine and sent me to the pharmacy to pick it up. Little did I know at that time, he also diagnosed me with Schizo-Affect.

I have no clue how I got to the pharmacy on base at the hospital and how I got myself back to the barracks. I also had no clue what Thorazine was. I accidentally overdosed and wound up nearly dead when my "Army mom" found me lying next to her bed. Apparently, I crawled from my room through our shared bathroom to her room looking for help.

She told me later she called emergency and an ambulance emergency crew came to rescue and rush me to the emergency room where my stomach was pumped. I had a Grand Mal Seizure. I had never had a seizure of any kind in my life up till then and since then. They strapped me down as I had this fight for my life growling like a bear and flipping in my body intensely like an outer body experience totally out of my control. When I woke after I am assuming a very long time, I felt intense confusion and anger for what happened and could not comprehend any of it. I did not know who I was, where I was and I was confused about everything. I was taken into Chambers, I don't remember details, but I do know that was the psychiatric hospital, the last place on base where anyone would ever want to go. I was so distraught and slept a lot because they had started treating me with more psychotropic drugs. At the time I did not know what any of these drugs were. Many years later I began to comprehend that the Staff Sergeant at the mental health clinic had diagnosed me with Schizo-Affect and this is the onset of me being diagnosed as having Schizophrenia. The truth is I was never Schizophrenic but this label has followed me and haunted me.

When I woke up in the Chamber's Hospital psychiatric ward there were strangers walking all around me just like in "One Flew Over the Cuckoo's Nest" movie. I could not comprehend where I was, what I was doing there, etc.

Zinha contacted my mother who was a biology teacher and had to up and fly to Texas to rescue me. Little did she know the military way of doing things. She just wanted to take me out of the hospital. I was so out of it I had no idea what was going on at the time since I was severely drugged and not all there. She told me years later it was a struggle to cut through all the DOD red tape. Had I known and was coherent I would have asked to be evaluated first for a medical discharge but no one tells you at the time and it is only years later to discover what really should have been done; "a medical evaluation to the findings of a disability while on active duty."

It has taken me a life time to figure out what happened to me. I still cry tears from time to time. I also learn more and more about myself and how my experience can help others. As a result, I have gained a lot of skills and compassion to help other people, mainly my veteran friends.

I feel extremely damaged by this entire mistake, yet I have become much stronger mentally, and emotionally. Physically I was pretty strong until more recent years after several surgeries and other health issues.

I have worked hard to overcome most of my insecurities and fears with tons of therapies and I still do this weekly. It is unfortunate this all happened and has taken my entire life to overcome and it altered it in ways I would never have expected, but I remind myself that things could be worse and that I would not be receiving the care I do now. I am forever grateful for the care I now receive at the Veteran Affairs in Martinez.

In 1976, I was evaluated at 100% service-connected disability. This rating was reevaluated a few times lowering my supports to the point I could not handle much after my divorce on my own.

A few years ago, I was reevaluated and my full 100% benefits were given back to me. I also have been diagnosed with Post Traumatic Stress Disorder (PTSD) and now receive help for this. I believe my Veteran Affairs benefits never should have been taken away from me if they understood PTSD, but at that time the Veteran Affairs did not understand PTSD or what I have been trying to deal with on my own.

I was determined to find a way to heal remembering how I was prior to joining the Army. I tried for years to put this trauma all in the past and pretend it never happened. I tried to run and hide, run and hide, run and hide. My panic and anxieties inevitably erupts when I try to hold it in...and I end up in a panic attack with tremendous anxiety that physically takes over my body. I shake and scream for help and waves of adrenaline swirl around my head and up and down my spine sending me spinning and running like a chicken with its head cut off. I hate it! Daily I attack my nails biting them till they bleed. I have literally bitten my entire nail bed unconsciously. I learned to hide, hide, hide...my lack of nails and weekly spent a lot of money getting nail tips put on professionally only to bite them off the next day and do it all over again. It was a vicious cycle. My anxieties have been persistent.

Did any of your struggles directly relate to the fact you are a female?

Perhaps indirectly, Yes.

Why would you say indirectly?

I believe that some women back then and perhaps even now are considered hysterical/mentally unstable by men. I cannot prove it. I just felt it. It has changed though now and I finally feel more supported by men as well as my women friends. I often feel misunderstood in general by many people. Over the years one VA psychiatrist treated me as if I were not even in his office. He asked questions while typing on his computer with barely a glance to look at me. I have learned to ask for what I need so I requested to see another psychiatrist. Now I love my psychiatrist and feel more empowered when I take charge of my life.

How did being in the military affect you as a person?

I am not at all the same person from the day I went in. I returned home very sick and traumatized. I needed a lot of help.

Now I receive so much more help and care from how it was in 1976. At first the treatment and care lacked the quality and understanding that we have today at the VA. Don't get me wrong...I loved my first therapist. She endured me flip flopping on her floor like a fish out of water. I shook all the time, and now realize it was all the drugs they put me on all along. I was never Schizophrenic. I just had insomnia and anxiety. The drugs exacerbated it.

I am more disciplined from my experience in the Army and I loved being there with and for my fellow soldiers with exception to the girls that taunted and attacked me. I love helping my fellow comrades now because I felt like such a failure for so long and now, I can give back my time. I feel like I never completed my duty and full commitment to my unit. I love helping all people but I gravitate to my fellow veterans.

Did you learn anything about yourself?

Completely! I was traumatized but I am also stronger for it. I am still learning more and more because the amnesia caused many gaps leaving me with a puzzle to figure out what happened.

After such a trauma we learn to be more resilient if we are to overcome hardships. I have struggled to fill in the blanks and learn how to settle and accept my confusion of who I am and what happened to me.

How have you changed since joining the military?

I suffer from panic and anxiety and for a very long time a feeling of not fitting into society. Trying to hide my traumatic experience from everyone and feeling guilty, afraid and worried that my panic will strike again and again.

I have a good life now because the VA now provides us with wonderful care and resources that truly help. I have had so much help understanding what happened and how I can cope with it...there are so many great ways to overcome much of my PTSD. I love to give back daily to other veterans, and to take my recreation group classes, painting, Equine therapy, ukulele, golfing, bowling, boat riding, trips, guitar for vets, and much more. We have many benefits shopping at the Exchange, and commissary, and other public support and discounts.

What would you tell women who are considering joining the military?

Just do whatever they tell you to do to the best of your ability during basic training and to speak up when there is a legitimate reason to do so thereafter.

Would you recommend they join the military or find another career path?

Absolutely! Despite what my experience turned out to be; my prior experience was so wonderful. I wish I could join again and again and even wish I stayed in for life...retirement!

What is your favorite memory from your military experience?

The camaraderie, uniforms, tough work, shooting my M16, cleaning it, night fire on automatic with tracers. Running, marching drills, singing, chanting, countdowns, gas bombs, digging trenches and putting up tents, learning how to camouflage ourselves and things, bivouac. And on and on...I love the military life! I wish I could do it all over again and make a career of it. 60 minutes came to film my platoon because they told us we were in the first Army group to shoot M-16s, lock and load them, clean them...etc. I wish I could find that taped show in the 60-minute archives. I have tried but without success so far.

*A*manda Wiley served in active duty in the Army. She left the army at the rank of Specialist (E4) to be a military spouse and stay at home mom.

Why did you decide to join the military?

I didn't want to go to college right away, and it would help pay for my college experience while letting me see the world and serve my country.

What was your career field/job?

I was a medical lab technician.

If you faced any difficulties did any of your struggles directly relate to the fact you are a female?

Yes. I had a fellow soldier decide it was ok to whip out his man parts while we were alone at work. I didn't stay silent about it and he got in trouble. Fortunately, it wasn't worse than that.

I also got pregnant while I was in and I decided to get out early to take care of my baby. I was likely going to deploy when my son would have been six or seven months old and I just couldn't handle the idea of being away from my baby. I know many women do serve while being mothers, but I just couldn't handle the idea.

That was one of the reasons I left the military as well. Was it hard to leave the military and to become a mom? Did you have any struggles with the transition?

Yes and no. It was hard to leave the Army in the sense that it was my life. It was surreal to go from being independent to being dependent on my new husband. I missed the camaraderie that I experienced in army life. It took a while to find other mom friends who I had anything in common with. The biggest struggle was letting someone else make the money. The first year I really struggled with feeling guilty about my husband paying all the bills. I could have worked, but when we looked into getting child childcare, I would have had to make a whole lot to make it worth doing, and I would have missed out on a lot with my son. We made the decision together that it made more sense for me to stay at home and raise our son. The part that was easy for me to leave the military was choosing my son over the army. I loved the Army, but I love my son more. It was an easy choice to get out so I wouldn't ever have to leave him. I know that there are lots of women who stay in and manage to survive deployments and separations from their families. I just don't think I could handle it.

How did being in the military affect you as a person? Did it change you? Did you learn anything about yourself?

Oh goodness... How can it not change you? I learned that I'm more capable than I had ever thought I was before. I think the hardest part was being away from everything I'd ever known and everyone I'd ever loved.

What would you tell women who are considering joining the military?

It's hard, but you can do it.

What is your favorite memory from your military experience?

Going to Korea and getting to experience life there.

How long were you in Korea?

I was in Korea twice for three weeks at a time. The unit I was in was very small, and they planned a mock deployment to Korea every spring.

What is your favorite memory from Korea?

The second time I went to Korea is when I met my husband. We had a weekend off, so we went to Busan and stayed in a nice hotel and walked on the beach and went to an aquarium. It was fun. Korea is a beautiful place.

What is the main difference you remember between Korea and the United States?

Traveling by train. In the States you don't get to travel by train often. You can of course but it's not a normal thing everyone does. In Korea that is a very normal way to travel.

If you are married, did your spouse serve while you were in/is he serving now?

I met my husband in Korea, and he is still serving.

How did you meet?

A friend of mine from Basic Training and AIT was stationed in Korea. I was hanging out with him and some of his friends when my now husband walked by. I thought he was cute, so I told him so. He ended up hanging out with us all weekend and the rest is history. :) We've been married almost 12 years now.

What was your transition in from your role in the military to military spouse?

In some ways, it is really nice having had my own army experience before becoming an army spouse. I know the army language and culture, so I understand what is going on and why my husband has to be away from us all the time. Like I said before, the hardest part for me was letting go of my own independence. It is humbling to let someone else pay for everything. My husband has always been very supportive of me staying home with our children though. He doesn't view his pay as only his, the money he makes is our money.

What is the hardest part of being a military spouse?

I think in a lot of ways being the military spouse is the harder job than being in the military. When you're the one serving you are busy all the time. Your mission is clear, you know what to do. Being a spouse and mother doesn't come with an SOP (standard operating procedure). You are often fighting the battles at home on your own because your spouse is always off doing the military thing. We joke that everything always goes bad the second they are away but it's so true. I get to handle all the house owner fun, vehicle maintenance, kids' drama, and anything else that comes along because my husband is either gone or getting ready to go and there isn't time for him to help with much of anything.

Have you gotten the chance to go back to school since leaving the military?

Yes. I started college when I was pregnant with my son and I graduated with my Bachelors in Science in Occupational Education when I was pregnant with my daughter (three years later).

*D*agmar Riley was a German citizen who married a service member who was stationed in Germany. She followed her husband to America, but it turned out not to be the best situation for her. He was an alcoholic who would leave her and children without food for days and she had to find a way to take care of her children. As a German citizen in America, she had a hard time finding a job. This led her to join the military. She served in the United States Army on active duty until she retired as a Sergeant First Class (E-7). During her career she was an Illustrator, Meteorological Observer, Transport Motor Vehicle Operator, and more.

Why did you decide to join the military?

My spouse was an alcoholic and often left me and my two children for days at a time without food and no phone or vehicle to call for help and we lived isolated away from town. I couldn't get a job anywhere because I was a German not American citizen and I had to find some way to provide for my children and so I joined the US Army in January 1979.

Wow. Did you meet your spouse when he was stationed overseas?

Yes, I met my first spouse while he was stationed in Germany where I'm originally from.

What is the process for you to join the military when you are a foreign national?

Actually, joining the military as a foreigner was no different than anyone else joining at that time; this might be different today. Once you reach the rank of E-5 and required a security clearance you needed to become a US Citizen. I applied for citizenship while in Advanced Individual Training (AIT) since I received orders for Europe to Shape HQ in Belgium and couldn't go there as a German citizen because of the high-security clearance requirements to work there.

Normally you need to be in the US for 5 years to become a citizen, but since I was in the military the requirement dropped down to three years. After my becoming a citizen I was cleared to make a Permanent Change of Station (PCS) to Europe but I got the assignment changed from Belgium to Germany since my stepfather was dying and my mother needed me for emotional support

Were you limited by any opportunities because you were a mom?

Yes, being a Mom did have its limitations. While stationed in Fürth, Germany, a recruiting team for a special unit contacted me to become a team member with this unit; very few soldiers in the Army were even eligible to join this unit, so it was a very high honor to even be contacted for this.

When my then husband found out about it and that I could be disappearing sometimes and he wouldn't know where I've gone he told me that he would leave me if I were to join this unit and so I had to turn it down because he did not want to be left alone with the children and something possibly could happen to me during a mission.

To this day I think that he reacted this way because he felt his ego bruised by not being the one that was selected for this. He often had a difficult time adjusting when I was able to do things he couldn't do, and I think that eventually tore our marriage to shreds. If he had left me, I still would not have been able to join that unit due to its mission and needing someone at all times for my children.

Where have you deployed to?

Wartime deployment to Saudi/Iraq/Kuwait during Desert

140

Shield/Storm.

What was you or your team's mission?

During Desert Shield/Storm my unit being in the Main Support Battalion (MSB), had the responsibilities of supporting the Forward Support Battalions (FSB) with whatever they needed to function in their support of the actual units fighting the battles.

We delivered rations, ammunition, fuel, parts and anything else that was necessary to them on a daily basis. My platoon ran convoys with food, water, parts, and mail to the FSB's daily. We often didn't get back to our unit until the early morning hours when everyone else was already asleep since we often had more than one Convoy to go and the later one usually didn't move out until sometime in the late afternoon hours.

What cultural differences do you remember between the country you went to and the United States?

The biggest cultural differences I saw was that women were supposed to make themselves invisible to men and not to even speak to a man unless spoken to. This could at times be a verbal confrontation since I was in charge of the convoy and I was cursed at on many occasions; didn't bother me one bit though. What was a bit more difficult was that the men could take off their shirt and work in the t-shirt when doing something very strenuous. But the women couldn't even roll our sleeves up without causing a major incident.

Did you face any challenges while you were deployed? If yes, what were they?

Some of the challenges I faced while deployed to Desert Shield/ Storm was the worry about my children since I knew that my husband was not very reliable at times and Family Support Groups were just started and were not functioning as well as most are today.

Other challenges were that shortly after moving out into the Desert, I was the only female in my platoon and when I got Reservists attached to my platoon, many were quite a bit older than I and did not appreciate a woman telling them what to do. After a few weeks though they realized that I did my job as well as any man there and that my troops that came with me fully stood behind me in everything I did, and it changed their attitude towards me somewhat.

Did you face any challenges while you were deployed because you were a female? If yes, what were they?

Another challenge I had was that often there were no other women in the Convoy (sometimes I had other women with me from another platoon). After a few hours driving people needed to take bathroom breaks, which usually was no challenge for the men at all. But it could be very challenging for me when there were no other women to look out for me since there were not any place to hide behind. All I could do is tell all my men to turn around so I could relieve myself and pray to God that they were gentlemen enough to give me the privacy needed like I did for them.

What was your career field/job?

I started out as an 81E (Illustrator) with first assignment to a Combat Engineer Brigade in Kornwestheim Germany, making charts and presentation slides for the Brigade Commanders Briefings to higher headquarters.

My Military Operation Specialty (MOS) code got phased out and I went back to school to become a 93E (Meteorological Observer). With my new job I got assigned to Headquarter Atmospheric Science Laboratory (ASL) at White Sands Missile Range (WSMR), New Mexico and collected and deciphered the data to provide data for the Air Defense Artillery (ADA) units in the area and also for the Space Shuttle whenever the possibility existed that it might have to land in our area which was a backup area if the weather prohibited landing in Florida.

This MOS also was phased out in the Army and I then became a 64C (Vehicle Operator) which later became known as 88M (Transportation Motor Vehicle Operator) and I drove mostly VIP's around and operated the big Commercial Buses (like the Greyhound buses) and drove children back and forth to Sports Activities in nearby Las Cruces where the children from Post went to school at.

After my assignment there I got stationed in the 2 Infantry Division at Camp Mobile, South Korea for a year. I started out as a driver there but after being there three months was moved into the orderly room as a clerk because they lost their clerk and couldn't get a replacement right away.

This assignment was followed by another assignment to Germany to 1st Trans Co in Fürth Germany and I again got stuck in the Orderly Room when the unit received a bad rating for their Personnel and Mailroom functions and fired the PSNCO they had. I still had to drive on top of that job though on weekends once or twice a month and somehow managed to win Personal Staff Non-Commissioned Officer (NCO) of the Quarter several times for the entire Community.

After I left there, I was assigned to Ft Hood Texas to the 1CD and actually got to drive again; for a while anyway. While assigned there I deployed to Desert Shield/Storm with my unit. While being there I worked as Convoy Commander since we didn't have enough Officers to go out as Convoy Commanders. We did see several dead bodies during those convoys and received artillery fire while out on Convoy; by the grace of God we never received any direct hits; all were near misses. During my time there I injured my back and so after returning back to Texas after our deployment I was sent to school again to become a Movement Control Specialist-88N and back to my unit until I got my orders for another tour in South Korea with the 8th Army this time being in charge of a Movement Control Team of military and civilian personnel in Waegwan at Camp Carroll.

This assignment was followed by another assignment at Fort Hood TX with the 2nd Armored Division this time actually working in my MOS still. After 3 years I went again to South Korea back to the 2nd Infantry Division (ID) at Camp Casey as a Movement Control NCO for the Division. After my year ended I went back to Ft Hood TX to the 4ID as a Movement Control NCO in the Division Support Command (DISCOM) and wrote a Movement Book for deployments since we did not have one and we wanted to prevent having the problems again when originally going to Desert Shield/Storm and were making up things as we went along.

Did you face any struggles while serving in the military?

When I got to my first unit a Combat Engineer unit I ran into a lot of sexual harassment when I first got there since I was only one of three women. After our first field exercise together though they learned quickly that I would work just as much if not more than some of the men and the guys in my unit started sticking up for me when a guy from another unit tried to harass me. That was probably one of the best units I ever served in.

I was also raped during one of my assignments in South Korea and attempted rape I was able to fight off while deployed to the Desert.

If you faced any difficulties did any of your struggles directly relate to the fact you are a female?

Each of my problems stemmed from being a woman because I had to always try to be better than my male counterparts to be accepted.

How did being in the military affect you as a person? Did it change you? Did you learn anything about yourself?

It made me a stronger person; gave me confidence in myself knowing that if I try hard enough, I can do just about anything I set my mind to. It also made me numb inside where often when I should feel something, I don't feel anything. I had a second marriage which also failed, and I've given up on relationships.

I have a difficult time relating around civilians and usually stay to myself. I do have a lot of friends though from my military career and even though I've been retired now since May 2000, I am still in touch online with many of my friends and once a year most of us try to come together for a reunion for a weekend.

What would you tell women who are considering joining the military?

Take care of yourself first because nobody else will but also always do your best in whatever you try to accomplish. Kind of like being in an airplane and the oxygen masks drop down and you need to put one on first or you can't be of help to others around you.

What is your favorite memory from your military experience?

There are so many and it's difficult to just pick one. I would have to say meeting so many wonderful people, seeing so many new places and I had so much fun spending a lot of time at a girl's orphanage in South Korea and spending time with them while enjoying BBQ's together and playing games giving them things they could otherwise not get and just being a friend to them.

Also, I have two Korean Families I've known and been friends with since my first tour in 1985, that I'm still in touch with and even have visited since retiring. They've always welcomed and taken me in like their own family.

What struggles did you have being married to someone also serving active duty?

I was married during my active duty time and my husband was

Amanda Huffman

active duty as well. He never deployed so during my deployments he found other things that drew his interest and he left me. I've seen dual military families that had no problems at all, but to many could not keep their marriage together from the ones I have met.

C *hristina served in the United States Army on active duty until she became pregnant with her oldest daughter. She missed military life and saw an opportunity to get back to the military lifestyle through the Army Reserves, which she joined when her daughter was about two years old. She serves is a Sergeant (E-5) in the Reserves and she currently works at the Alliance Laundry Systems as a Transportation Coordinator.*

Why did you decide to join the military?

I wanted to do something with my life, and growing up in a military family, so it just seemed like the right choice.

When and where have you deployed to?

2011-2012, Kuwait

What was your rank when deployed?

Private First Class (E-3), then to Specialist (E-4)

What was your team's mission while you were deployed?

There were three parts to our mission.

The first part was to go around to the different areas of Kuwait and make sure the contractors were doing their job right.

The second part (which I was involved with) was working with the Kuwaiti army in scheduling and verifying transportation routes (convoys).

The third was LSA (airport), we were in charge of head count and get soldiers to the plane so they could go home on Rest and Recuperation (R&R).

What differences do you remember from the United States and

Amanda Huffman

Kuwait?

In Kuwait there is no speed limit, or seatbelt laws, also you are not allowed to interfere with an accident.

Is there any memory from your deployment you would want to share?

We were driving to our post for the night and there was a horrible accident (at least a five-car pile-up), bodies all over the highway on the right-hand side. I had asked my Staff Sergeant (E-6) if we were going to stop and help, he said no. That if we did, we would be arrested. In Kuwait it's all about religion. He said that if Allah wanted the people to die than it shall be.

What was your career field/job?

Military Operation Specialty (MOS): 88N- Transportation Coordinator. My job was to get materials from point A to point B.

What type of material?

Containers, Soldiers and equipment.

Did you face any struggles while serving in the military?

No, not really. Because, I can easily adapt to my environment it was easy for me to conform to men within my unit. I wasn't easily offended either, because of my background.

What part of military life might offend some females that you were able to ignore?

When you work around men (a lot), you have to adapt too. I wasn't sexually harassed, but I had to become "one of the guys". They respected me and I respected them.

If you faced any difficulties did any of your struggles directly relate to the fact you are a female?

Some, but I was able to handle it and resolve the issues fast.

What sort of experiences were you able to overcome?

I used to have a fear of the sound of gunshots, but of course I don't now.

How did being in the military affect you as a person? Did it change you? Did you learn anything about yourself?

It taught me responsibility and gave me a sense of pride that only the military could give. It made me a stronger person by integrating the morals of 1,000's of soldiers before me.

What would you tell women who are considering joining the military?

Do it!! It was the best choice career-wise I've ever made.

What is your favorite memory from your military experience?

The friends that I have made.

If you are married, did your spouse serve while you were in/is he serving now?

Both my husband and I served (he is still serving), as of right now we live in Ripon, WI and he teaches ROTC at the college here.

How did you meet your husband?

We met at Advanced Individual Training (AIT) right after boot camp, he was the first guy to say "Hi" lol, we met and married in three months and we've been married for twelve years.

Do you struggle with being a military spouse after serving in the military?

No, I'm used to it and can switch between him being around and not.

L *yndsey served in the United States Army on both active duty and the National Guard. She is a blogger at dearlyndsey.com and is finally finished the process of leaving the military through a Medical Board from an injury that took place in 2016. She is now medically retired and focuses on her blog and her family. She was a 31B which is a Military Police (MP) officer. Military police officers patrol the base and answer calls that come in. She retired as a Specialist (E-4).*

Why did you decide to join the military?

I joined so I could provide for my family and to prove that I could make something of myself. I wasn't confident in myself and had a decent amount of insecurities. I also wanted that sense of security from having a stable career.

Why did you switch from Active Duty to National Guard?

When I got pregnant with my son, I decided to switch so I could stay home with him. It was a pretty easy transition for me thankfully I had decent Non-Commissioned Officers (NCOs) that helped with the process. The hardest part was getting to my guard unit and transferring to a new state in the guard.

Do you have any interesting stories from your patrols as a MP?

I have one. A man went into one of the base houses to steal things from the home. Well, he happened to pass out on the couch in that house. The owner living there had to call us since the guy was still passed out on their couch. It makes me laugh every time.

Did you face any struggles while serving in the military?

Yes, learning to balance my job and my family. As an MP my

schedule was different than others and I had to learn how to try and balance time with my family while finding time to rest for the different shifts.

What ways did you find balance?

It was very hard but getting on a schedule helped. Since I was an MP our schedules were different when I was on different shifts. So, I would have to make time to sleep and time to spend with my family. We slowly figured out what worked for us schedule wise.

How did being in the military affect you as a person? Did it change you? Did you learn anything about yourself?

Yes, it showed me that I can be independent and that I can tackle anything that is thrown at me. I learned that I have to get over my fears and sometimes just do things that life is entirely too short to be caught up on what ifs or I should have done that.

What would you tell women who are considering joining the military?

I would tell them that they should do it and hold their head high. It is an honor to work alongside other strong women. We all need to stick together and that you should be ready for an adventure. It is such a rewarding career and take every opportunity that you can to travel through the branch you choose.

What is your favorite memory from your military experience?

My favorite memories are the friends that I have gained over the years. I also got to experience flying in a Blackhawk and Chinook. This was huge for me because I have a fear of heights. But it was such a wonderful adrenaline rush.

If you are married, did your spouse serve while you were in/is he serving now?

My spouse served before me. He was medically retired from the

Amanda Huffman

Army when I decided to join.

Did he support your choice to join the military?

Yes, he supported me 100% I couldn't have asked for a better spouse to back me in that career path. It also helped that he was prior military so he knew all the crazy things that can come up and what I would have to put up with.

*M*oniek James-Eldridge served in the United States Army on Active Duty. She worked in the Intelligence community and served overseas in Korea. She left the Army at the rank of Staff Sergeant (E-6) and is currently an entrepreneur, the owner of Confetti Collective and Renegade Creative Media Group

Why did you decide to join the military?

I needed to make a radical change in my life, and joining the Army was there.

What was your career field/job?

Cryptologic Linguist

What does that mean? What are the main duties or why is your job important to the military?

It's an intelligence position. A cryptologic linguist is primarily responsible for identifying foreign communications using signals equipment. Their role is crucial as the nation's defense depends largely on information that comes from foreign languages.

Have you deployed? If yes, where?

Does Korea count? If so, yes.

What was your job while you in Korea?

I worked in the intelligence industry.

What was the hardest part of being in Korea?

I loved it! I enjoyed the adventure, if I had to pick a "hard part" it was my work schedule. I rotated between day and night shift.

Did you experience any differences between the culture of the

US and Korea? What were they?

I was prepared for the differences and I knew the language so it helped overcome the initial culture shock.

What is your favorite memory(ies) from Korea?

I made friends that I still have today, we're actually planning a vacation for next year together.

Did you face any struggles while serving in the military?

I dealt with the physical challenges of transitioning from civilian to soldier, and during my linguist training I had to find my own rhythm in order to complete my training.

If you faced any difficulties did any of your struggles directly relate to the fact you are a female?

It would be easy to say that adapting to a rigorous physical activity schedule was because of my gender, but I served with women in basic training that were powerhouses during Physical Training. They actually inspired me to try harder and do my best every day.

How did being in the military affect you as a person? Did it change you? Did you learn anything about yourself?

I attribute my success as an entrepreneur to my time as a soldier. Not only did I learn the discipline and dedication to duty that guides me in my business, but I actually discovered my confidence as a woman while being a soldier. I was challenged by my chain of command, put into positions that I didn't think I could do, and when I succeeded, I learned that I could accomplish whatever I set out to do.

What is your business?

I own The Confetti Collective, a lifestyle platform that inspires confidence in women and girls through live events, online content and inspirational jewelry. I also own Renegade Creative

Media Group, a consulting agency that specializes in social media training and brand experiences.

Why did you decide to leave the military?

I left the military in 2007 after the birth of our daughter. My husband retired in early 2018 after 22 years.

How were you able to make an adjustment from civilian life to military life?

I had my sister. She'd transitioned out of the military a few years before I did so she filled in the gaps that the Army Transition Program didn't cover.

What would you tell women who are considering joining the military?

I would tell them to first prepare their bodies! The journey will be less challenging if they're not nursing injuries. I would tell them to pursue the hard thing, instead of turning away. Take advantage every opportunity they can, especially furthering their education.

Is there any piece advice you would give to a female considering joining the military?

Make a plan for your life before you enlist. Decide how the military will be an avenue for your next chapter, and be great.

What is your favorite memory from your military experience?

The adventures; every new duty station was an adventure. I met battle buddies that became friends then family. Joining the military was the best decision I could have made; it changed my life for the better.

If you are married, did your spouse serve while you were in/is he serving now?

My husband and I met while on active duty. We've been married for 15 years now, he retired at the beginning of 2018.

How did you meet your husband?

We met in the military; we were in the same unit.

How did life change when you married your spouse?

It didn't. Getting married was something we talked about, we went to pre-marital counseling and decided that we would tackle everything together. 15 years later we're still a team.

What is it like to be a dual military couple?

It's interesting, we fell in sync almost organically. Since we were in the same unit, we learned early that we needed our own space so we drove to work separately.

What challenges do you face while both serving in the military?

Once our daughter was born, we had to decide who would be the primary parent, and accepted that one of us would have to leave the military if we were deployed.

What is the hardest part of being a dual military couple?

Taking off the soldier when we both get home. My husband out-ranked me but I was in a leadership position, we had to train ourselves to be husband and wife once we left work.

NAVY

*S*andra served in the United States Navy on Active Duty and is currently serving in the Reserves and works as a Port Engineer for the National Oceanic and Atmospheric Administration (NOAA). She is a Lieutenant Commander (LCDR) (O-4).

Why did you decide to join the military?

This is a story all by itself. I had always been fascinated with flying and space as a child and was an avid Trekkie. The basic plan was join the Navy, fly jets, become an astronaut. My family was not encouraging of this idea, in fact my father was and is epically anti-military. Despite having no way to fund my college education, his reaction to my mentioning that I was considering applying to the Naval Academy was an epic 2-hour rant on the side of the highway. Needless to say I did not apply to the Naval Academy, instead I enrolled at the University of Michigan, studying Naval Architecture and Marine Engineering, with the intent of designing racing yachts, my other passion at the time.

I had financial aid in the form of various loans and a few grants. I paid for books and incidentals by working as a sailing instructor, washing dishes, hauling traps on a lobster boat, and tutoring. My father was laid off my sophomore year and could no longer co-sign the loans, nor was there anyone else in my family who met the income requirements. My grandmother was living off my grandfather's pension, which although she was able to regularly sent me $50.00 or so, was not enough for the bank. My mother's only income was disability benefits from social security. It was only $6,000 that I needed a co-signer for, but when you don't have it, that is a lot of money.

I figured I would go to sea as a merchant seaman, earn enough in six to seven months to cover a year's tuition, and return after a sailing season. I wanted to sit for the Coast Guard exam for Able Seaman as I already had some sea time. Passing the exam would grant me slightly higher pay and make it more likely I would find a position in the first place. To take the exam, I needed to show I had a course on cargo handling.

My Intro to Marine Design course had covered ship loading and stability in detail and I had excelled in the class, receiving a nearly perfect grade. I asked the professor for a letter of recommendation. Much to my surprise, my professor said no. After I laid out why I was planning to leave school, he argued was that I was too good a student to just walk away, that once I started earning real money as a merchant sailor, I would find it more difficult to return to school than I anticipated. He offered to work with the department and the college to find a way to allow me to stay and graduate. He was much more certain than I was that there was a better way forward.

About a week after that conversation, and with no good solutions in hand and the tuition for the next semester coming due, I stopped by a booth at a student fair where Air Force ROTC was recruiting, and I signed up for an interview. The interview was very straight forward, I was asked what my major was, what hobbies and interested I had, and how I spent my summers. The interviewing officer, an Air Force Captain was somewhat bemused by my answers; Naval Architecture and Marine Engineering, maintenance director for the sailing team, sailing instructor and boatswain on a 150 ft schooner. The he wryly asked me if I had met the people across the hall . . . . with the anchors on their collars, proceeded to walk me over to the Navy ROTC unit, introduce me to the unit Commander by saying he felt we might have a lot to talk about, and left me standing there somewhat nervously.

That say set the course for the next thirteen years of my life. The Navy had a unique scholarship, given to one student a year who was not otherwise eligible for a NROTC scholarship . . .that year I got it. About two weeks later, the Naval Architecture Department also gave me a $6000.00 merit scholarship, and allowed me to keep it despite the Navy support. My professor believed that between academics and NROTC I wouldn't have time for a student job. He was right, to graduate on the time table the Navy wanted, with the extra courses they required, I was often taking 22-24 credits per semester in contrast to the 15-18 that usually made up a full-time course load.

Have you deployed? If yes, where?

I deployed twice at sea aboard USS KAUFFMAN (FFG-59), we did anti-narcotic operations in the Caribbean and Central America, circumnavigated South America while escorting USS GEORGE WASHINGTON (CVN 73) for part of her transit from Virginia to Japan, passed through the Panama Canal several times, and delivered United States Agency for International Development (USAID) supplies to multiple countries, as well as participated in several multinational exercises.

As a reservist I responded to a request for engineering and acquisitions support to the USS JOHN S MCCAIN (DDG 56) collision and spent six months in Yokosuka, Japan as the Business Manager for the project.

What was your job while you were deployed?

I filled several different roles in my time abroad the KAUFFMAN. Initially I was assigned as Electronics Maintenance Officer but for the majority of tour aboard I was in the auxiliaries and main propulsion divisions. I stood watches on the bridge as Conning Officer or Officer of the Deck, was a member of the At Sea Fire Party, ran the Morale Welfare and Recreation Program and primarily did what most junior officers do, which is focus on getting qualified.

In contrast to most of my colleagues I loved being assigned to engineering divisions. Over the course of a two-year assignment this meant that I had a rough idea of what was required to fix almost every piece of equipment on the ship. The troubleshooting and hands-on skills I learned from my enlisted sailors, especially the Chief Engineman, I still use in my civilian job.

What deployment was the most memorable?

My first deployment was the most memorable. Everything was new, I had never been to the ports we were visiting, every port call was a chance to see new things, try new foods, learn a little bit about a new place. Every exercise or shipboard operation was a chance to learn something new. None of it was routine yet.

What was the hardest part of being deployed?

The hardest part of deployment was dealing with family at home who simply did not understand that email connections were sporadic, that I really couldn't call, and that I wasn't homesick. My time aboard KAUFFMAN had challenges but few of them were specific to being deployed.

Did you experience any differences between the culture of the US and the various countries you visited? What were they?

Each country, each city has its own flavor. I can't think of any big surprising cultural differences, but I grew up as a first generation American and generally find other cultures more interesting than shocking.

Most of the foreign Navies we dealt with were surprised I was an officer and an engineer, but then again that made me a rarity in the US Navy as well.

In Chile avocado is a very common condiment. In Peru people eat a meat and corn rich soup for breakfast and kids go to school in shifts. I love food and trying new things, I could probably name a food I had for the first time in each port.

What is your favorite memory from the deployment?

Definitely SCUBA diving in Belize, the coral was amazing, and the reef was full of fish as it was in few of the other ports we visited.

Did you face any challenges deployed because you were a female?

My first ship was a lonely assignment, I was either the only female aboard or one of two in a command of over 200. There were several senior enlisted onboard who believed women didn't belong at sea on warships, an issue that had been settled when I was in the fourth grade. Frigates such as KAUFFMAN had no female enlisted aboard, and for the majority of my tour I was the only female officer. When there were two of us things were not necessarily better. My roommate and I were very different people, she was much more traditionally feminine, and I had senior officers who thought nothing of telling me that I would do better if I wore make-up routinely, or dressed up more to leave the ship, the way she did. She was assigned as the Training Officer and often worked in our air conditioned state room, I was assigned to engineering and was often in machinery spaces that were over 100 degrees. It was nearly impossible to stay clean doing my job and nearly impossible to get dirty doing hers. I was nearly constantly admonished for this.

One particularly memorable incident was while the ship was dead in the water due to unusual noises from the vicinity of the main reduction gear (MRG). We had two gas turbine engines, one main reduction gear, and one shaft. The MRG was potentially a single point of failure in our propulsion train and was kept locked. I had just finished inspecting the MRG for damage, a procedure that required securing the area and posting a guard, stripping off anything that could fall in the gears and damage them such as rings, watches or hair pins, taping over the buttons on my coveralls. I could not have my hair pinned up, I tied it back in a clean rag to keep it out of my face and out of the MRG as it was slowly rotated. I had completed the inspection and was in the process of closing the water tight door to the main engine room when the Operations Officer decided that he needed to take the time to voice his thoughts on the general state of my coveralls (somewhat oily with take over the buttons), hair (tied in a rag), face (red and sweaty from the 106 degree heat in the space) and general disposition (more concerned with the state of the vessel than the fact that I had oil on my knees). The ship was dead in the water with a potentially crippling engineering casualty, barely holding position on the Gulf Stream with its auxiliary propulsion units, and the state of the Main Propulsion Assistant uniform was more important to the Operation's Officer than the information she may have to convey. It is an attitude I still cannot comprehend, and I doubt a male officer would have been asked about anything other than the state of his equipment in such a circumstance.

I am not, and never was, a big drinker. Between the sexual discrimination that was a matter of course, and the heavy drinking culture I did not often socialize with the other officers in the wardroom (a commissioned officers mess onboard a warship). We had little in common with each other. After a few incidents where some of them thought it was OK to steal my laundry and comment on my undergarments, loudly discuss my attractiveness (or lack thereof) in front of several sailors in my division, or hide my qualification books, I did not trust most of them.

In order to go off the ship I needed a liberty buddy unless I was on an organized tour. I often got off the ship by going on the tours that I had set up as the morale, welfare, and recreation officer. In Chile and Peru, the guides who worked for the tour company we had contracted were two young women about my age. I often went with them on a "one-person tour" in the evenings. It wasn't quite by the book, and a few people knew what was happening...but otherwise I would have essentially been confined to the ship and certainly going out with two young women who were native to the country we were visiting was safer than going out with my shipmates, where I wasn't welcome anyway.

Where gender never mattered to the people around me when I was racing sailboats, pulling lobster traps, or hauling sails on a schooner, it seemed to be the most important thing about me to the Surface Navy, and my interest and aptitude for engineering put me firmly at odds with what most of the senior personnel around me thought a female officer should be like. Since that first tour I have been in assignments with the engineering duty community where I was the only woman in the room, or one of only two or three at the command. There the focus was on my professional knowledge and my ability to do the job, my gender made me memorable perhaps, but it was not the focus of the people around me the way it was during those first few years.

What was it like to be on a ship while deployed? Living conditions? Male to female ratio? Food?

A ship is like a small village with all the good and bad that can come with a small isolated community. When underway you just fall into a rhythm, meals are the major events that mark watch turn over and the beginning and end of the work day. Often you stand watches in a rotating cycle and are both too busy and too sleep-deprived to do much besides work, study for qualifications, and sleep.

As a junior officer on a ship I had a three-person stateroom, the bunks are three high and there is not quite enough room to sit up in bed. I had several lockers to store my things in and a small desk that folded down from one of the lockers. It was enough space for what I needed, I even managed to bring my violin and SCUBA gear, but then again, I only packed a few changes of civilian clothes.

The food is not bad, more or less like what you get in a cheap restaurant. Once away from the US the ship buys a lot of its provisions in foreign ports so we would get the local version of hot sauce, some tropical fruits along with more familiar staples. Sometimes the cooks had no idea what to do with it, once the simply dumped a box of passion fruit in the salad bar for people to eat, not knowing that it is not eaten the way an apple is. We had a few cooks that really loved being cooks, they would bake bread underway, a scent that traveled throughout the ship on the midnight watch, they would also look up recipes and have fun with the varied provisions we received.

Is there a difference between deploying while on active duty and as a reservist?

When you deploy on active duty you are deploying as a team with others from your command. You are all away from home and family, you all have little else to focus on outside the mission, and you generally socialize together in your off time.

As a reservist in my field, I will almost always go to a shore command, usually a shipyard or regional maintenance center. Not only do I walk in the door as the outsider at the command but while everyone else has homes and families to go home to, all their regular routines and activities, I am entirely on my own. It is isolating and lonely in a way I wasn't really expecting. I am the outsider who it is presumed will not be around long enough to really be worth knowing.

It is also hard because my paperwork is a little bit different so everything from pay issues to changes in my orders to travel is twice as hard as it should be. I've been told after eleven years of service that I don't exist in the medical or pay system because the person looking was not familiar with how reservist records are set-up.

What was your career field/job?

I was and still am an Engineering Duty Officer (EDO). I started as

Amanda Huffman

a Surface Warfare Officer (ship driver) and transferred into the EDO community to specialize in ship maintenance and acquisition after 5 years. I qualified in nuclear maintenance at Portsmouth Naval Shipyard and have significant experience with various platforms from fast attack submarines, to deep submergence vessels, to survey ships.

I do the same work as a civilian for the National Oceanic and Atmospheric Administration where I plan and oversee ship maintenance and modernization for a hydrographic survey vessel staffed by the NOAA commissioned Corps. I consider myself very lucky in that I am still serving an important mission and working with great colleagues who value my skill...I just get to choose my clothes each morning.

Did you face any struggles while serving in the military?

I am often the only woman everywhere I go. My first ship was miserable and isolating and the sexual harassment and discrimination were rampant and blatant. I am also not naturally athletic; I am rather clumsy and get injured easily so I struggle with forced group PT (and usually get injured). I found my niche in the engineering duty world, as a surface warfare officer I was too smart, too clumsy, too often in engineering with oil on my coveralls, too soft spoken, too caring towards my sailors...etc.

If you faced any difficulties did any of your struggles directly relate to the fact you are a female?

Most of my struggles were due to being female in a heavily male environment and that environment only valuing one way of being. The maintenance community cares only that I know my profession and do my job well...in this field being the only female can be a bonus, everyone knows who I am, and people usually remember me.

How did being in the military affect you as a person? Did it change you? Did you learn anything about yourself?

166

I learned to be more comfortable speaking in public, I learned to stand up for myself more and to have confidence in my judgement. I learned to make decisions on the fly and to stick to my guns when people question me. I learned that being confident in how you deliver information is at least as important as being right.

What would you tell women who are considering joining the military?

Do it. Own it. You will always stand out and people will always tell you, you don't belong, don't let them stop you or change you.

So much of what I have written here is about the hard stuff, but my time in service was about so much more than that. There were moments of joy, beauty, triumphant accomplishment, camaraderie and friendship. Sunsets and storms at sea, exploring various ports, late nights chatting with colleagues from all over the country, pulling the ship alongside a pier for the first time, trading sea stories with Italian or Japanese naval officers, writing repair estimates that were passed directly to Congress, dry docking a submarine, signing off on a plan for manned testing of a deep submergence vehicle, helping a sailor get home for his grandfather's funeral or the birth of his first child. There is the fact that I received the six years of university education and countless hours of professional training that allow me to work as a senior engineer in a field I love.

I would make the same choice to join the Navy all over again.

What is your favorite memory from your military experience?

I have two. One is about the sheer beauty of being at sea. I miss the sunrises, the photoluminescence glowing in the ship's wake and most of all, standing on the bridge wing of a ship at sea and looking up at the stars. The night sky, when you are far enough away from land to escape the light pollution, is an amazing sight.

My other favorite memory comes from a moment of struggle. I was newly reported to the shipyard in Kittery, ME. It was something of a special assignment, I was neither a nuclear trained officer nor a submariner, and the shipyard specialized in submarine repair. I had however grown up about 45 minutes away, and as the newly single mother of a two-year-old had asked the Navy to station me there so that I would family to help with childcare. My ex had followed me to the area and had base access as a veteran. Through whatever contacts he had made he had managed to call the command and complain that I was not qualified for my job and imply that I had cheated the system to get my orders.

The truth was I had asked and after consulting with the shipyard commander, the Navy had said yes . . .but once I heard about the complaints, I was doubting myself and my place at the shipyard. A fellow officer, who had been tasked with helping me learn the ropes in the shipyard, had heard about the complaints through the grapevine and picked up on my self-doubt. He proceeded to pull me aside and layout all my accomplishments to date and read me the riot act about even thinking of letting something so inane knock me off my course. His take was that I belonged in the shipyard if I thought I belonged in the shipyard and clearly the commanding officer agreed. For the next many weeks, he helped me study submarine systems and nuclear engineering, and made sure I knew where to get the answers to any other topics I was struggling with. His support in those first few weeks and his friendship throughout that tour kept me afloat when I was struggling.

If you are married, did your spouse serve while you were in/is he serving now?

I am not married. I am single with a seven-year-old son, my relationship fell apart on active duty and in many ways the nasty custody battle that followed, cost me my regular commission as it took SO MUCH TIME AND ENERGY, I failed to finish some critical qualifications before a promotion board as was not selected for the next rank while on active duty. The Navy changed its mind seven months later and promoted me as a reservist three days after I separated from active service. Letting my ex get the better of me by being a distraction is one of the few things I truly regret.

My partner was supportive when I was struggling during my tours as a surface warfare officer, but couldn't handle it when I went to graduate school and my career starting taking off. The straw that broke the camel's back was our son was about ten months old. My ex had taken several jobs as a yacht mechanic that kept him out of the house during the work week. He would come home on Friday evening, trash the house and spend most of the weekend watching TV, sleeping, or drinking.

The baby and the house were my job. I was juggling a full course load as a graduate student and our son had started walking. . . .and getting into everything. I could not get any homework done while he was awake unless he was at daycare or my neighbor's daughter was watching him. I was sleeping maybe two to three hours a night between taking care of the house, the baby, and trying to get all my school work done.

I had requested that the Navy allow me to withdraw from one course of the five courses I was taking and extend my tour at the Naval Postgraduate School by three months. The course had a project that was primarily done out of class and I was ridiculously far behind. It had taken an enormous amount of prodding from my neighbors to get me to muster up the courage to ask my program officer for the extension, and it had taken the vote of the entire mechanical engineering faculty to have the extension granted.

My ex's reaction when I told him that the Navy had granted my request was to tell me that I had "pulled a mommy card" and that I was clearly over my head and unable to compete. I had until that term had a 3.8 GPA. I had not taken a real maternity leave, instead taking two course the term my son was born and returning to class within three days after giving birth. I decided that day that I did not need someone in my life who would not support and help me and who saw my success as a threat to his self-worth. It was one of the best decisions I ever made.

MARINES

*S*usan Smith Parrish served in the United States Marine Corps on Active Duty and reached the rank of Corporal (E-4). The military required her to leave the service when she became pregnant with her first child. After leaving the military she worked for 30 years at the Veterans Administration and is now retired.

Why did you decide to join the military?

My Dad was a Navy Chief and my three older brothers were all "lifers", so I thought it was the only thing to do.

What was your career field/job?

I was an Aviation Storekeeper stationed at Fleet Marine Force Atlantic in Norfolk, VA. Small base, Camp Elmore. It was my job to prepare requisitions for equipment, one bolt at a time. LOL

What type of equipment?

Since I was an Aviation Storekeeper my job was to prepare requisitions for anything related to Aviation. This included all types of aircraft, ammunition or any equipment needed by one of our Marine Air Groups. The running joke was that we started with nuts and bolts and ended with an airplane or helicopter. Most of the airplanes back in the good ol' days were propeller driven and not as sleek as the jets of today.

Did you face any struggles while serving in the military?

No. I was fortunate to serve in small group. The male Marines were very accepting of the females and treated us with a great deal of respect.

How did being in the military affect you as a person? Did it change you? Did you learn anything about yourself?

Since I was raised in a military environment, I did not relate to being a civilian. I did not know there were female nurses until I was discharged. I had been seen by corpsmen most of my life. I don't think the military changed me much. I learned I could be an independent female responsible for her own future.

What would you tell women who are considering joining the military?

I would tell them it is one of the best ways to become a woman who is in charge of her own destiny. My great-granddaughter is currently in AFJROTC and I have encouraged her to follow this course for the future.

What is your favorite memory from your military experience?

There are many. I think the most outstanding memory was receiving the Eagle, Globe and Anchor (EGA) and knowing I was one of the few. I was the only Marine in our family and I never let my brothers forget it.

What does EGA stand for?

EGA is Eagle, Globe and Anchor, the Marine Corps emblem. When I finished Boot Camp, standing in formation with my sister "Boots" I was given the emblem and during that one second became a Marine. I do not know how to adequately describe that feeling. I really think you have to be one to know one. I think it is something instilled in us during Boot Camp. We are truly the few.

Why did you choose the Marines after having a long line of military service in the Navy?

Since my formative years were spent on Naval Air Station, Corpus Christi, Texas, I knew very little of civilian life. I thought it was natural to be in the military. So, when I visited the recruiting office with my Dad the discussion was "what branch". After taking the exams the recruiter, who knew my family history, suggested the Marine Corps. He said my test scores qualified me and told Dad he would have a child in four different branches. He thought my oldest brother was still Army. Our hometown newspaper ran an article headlined as "Chief Smith gives last child to Uncle

If you are married, did your spouse serve while you were in/is he serving now?

I married a fellow Marine who was soon to be discharged. When we became pregnant, I had no choice to remain in the Corps as that was not allowed at the time. The day my discharge came through, the Commander told me my orders to Hawaii arrived also. My husband said he would have reupped if I could have stayed in the Corps as his MOS would have probably warranted a billet in Hawaii also. But we both returned to his hometown, raised three children and remained married until his death 42 years later.

When you served in the Marines you were forced to leave when you had children?

Females were not allowed to remain in the Marines if they were pregnant. I do not know the date this was changed. I cannot answer for my husband, but I certainly would have stayed if I had been allowed to.

How did you meet your late husband?

My future husband was also stationed on the small base, Camp Elmore, Virginia. There was a small club, The Slop Chute, where we all visited almost every night. Beer was cheap, the burgers were good, and it was easier to go there than to make the long trek to main side Norfolk or to go downtown where the civilians hated the military. He was a great dancer and one of the few who could still be on his feet after several beers. He was in Motor Transport and I was in Service Command so the only time we saw each other was at the "Chute". So, we spent most of our evenings together.

Did you struggle with the transition to civilian life after leaving the military?

When we arrived at his hometown after discharge, he returned to his former job and I became a Mom. We bought a house and I worked as a grocery cashier and doctors' receptionist until I took the Civil Service Exam which ultimately lead to my job at the Veteran Affairs (VA). I do not think I had a struggle with returning to civilian life. Actually, I do not think I was ever really a civilian. Since he was also a Marine, our life still seemed as regimented. And, at that time, the VA seemed to be more like military employment.

What was your experience working in the Veteran Affairs after serving in the military?

I started with the Veteran Affairs as a Clerk Typist, GS-3. This was a great job at that time with excellent pay and benefits as compared to the private sector. I was fortunate to advance in this career. I became a Veterans Claims Examiner and then a Rating Specialist, GS-12. From there I was promoted to Rating Board Section Chief, GS-13 and retired from that position because my husband has already retired from his job and wanted me to join him at our fish camp.

Have your kids followed the military tradition your family has?

My son had considered joining the Corps, but his best friend was a Marine brat and told my son he would be making a big mistake. When he told me that I realized he was not really a candidate for the Marines. My oldest daughter occasionally spoke of going into the Air Force because they offered a career field in which she was interested. Since she did not press the issue, I felt she was not really serious about it and that she was not a good candidate either. My younger daughter married soon after

High School, so she had no interest in leaving her husband for any reason. However, she did interest and aptitude for work at the VA. So, she started as a Clerk Typist, GS-4 in the Finance Division. When I retired, she was able to transfer to the Division from which I left. She worked her way up to Rating Specialist and is looking forward to her retirement in two years.

The only grandchildren of "The Chief" who joined the military were the son and daughter of my youngest brother, also a Navy Chief. Son joined the Marines; Daughter joined the Navy.

CONCLUSION

After working to collect these stories I was led to start a podcast called Women of the Military. If you want to hear more stories of military women you can check it out here.

Thank you for reading. If you enjoyed the book leave a review on Amazon and tell your friends. This book is meant to be a resource for those looking to join the military. And I also hope to help people learn about all the work women are doing in the military. You can also email me at airmantomom@gmail.com if you would like to be interviewed for a future version of this book or to be a guest on the podcast.

Thank you so much.

Amanda

*Name changed for privacy

Made in the USA
Middletown, DE
23 November 2019

79288301R00111